Towards a
Planetary
Vision

DAVID SPANGLER

FINDHORN

© 1977 David Spangler
First published 1977
Second edition 1980

ISBN 0 905249 49 6

Designed by Shari Mueller and Hilary Baird
Illustrations by Alice Rigan
Calligraphy by Leeya Thompson

Set in 10/12 Theme Medium
Printed, bound and published by
Findhorn Publications
The Park, Forres IV 36 OTZ, Scotland.

To understand the creation of this book is to understand how Findhorn works. When an assignment is accepted, total trust is given to that individual to see it through to completion using whatever resources he or she feels appropriate. And so it was with me. Overseeing the transference of these lecture transcripts into book form was a new experience for me. All fell into place easily—except the challenge of illustration. In meditation I was met with silence. Later, on a week's retreat at the community's home on the western Scottish isle of Iona, after Ireland, Christianity's first home in Britain, I again asked for guidance on the illustration for *Towards a Planetary Vision*. This time I was shown a book with Celtic knotwork designs and an image of people joining hands, creating a chalice to support the planet. This was the answer, but the question of who could carry out the vision was still a mystery. We needed to manifest a graphic artist who could do this style of illustration and I constantly reminded myself that by the laws of manifestation, your needs will be met if you are working in harmony with the whole.

The day I returned from Iona, Alice Rigan arrived at Findhorn. When she came into publications to help collate papers, we discovered that she was a designer and was delighted to stay and work on the illustrations, although she had no previous experience with Celtic art.

The end of the story is the product of this book through the synthesis of two people's energies and a willingness to attempt something new.

The Celtic symbol in the centre of each chapter page is symbolic of the contents of that chapter. 'Celtic Art' is the original art of Europe and the British Isles, a sacred language linked with the mystery traditions of early cultures both East and West, built around symbols to be found everywhere from China to South America, from the Antipodes to the Arctic. Adapted by the early Celtic Christian communities of Iona and Lindisfarne in Roman times, the form reached perfection as a graphic art to illuminate the spiritual impulse towards a planetary vision.

Linked to a revelation of the ageless wisdom and coming from a group consciousness pioneering new cultural values, Celtic art in its original spirit is a synthesis of universal symbolism and traditional discipline with spontaneity, humour and simplicity. Findhorn shares this vision.

Shari Mueller
Findhorn, 1977

Introduction

The lectures on which this book is based were given by David Spangler to the Findhorn community as sharing his vision at the time of the new age into which man is entering.

They are issued now in this more permanent form, not because they are thought to give an authoritative or final statement of truth, but simply in the faith that they may have the same inspiring and stimulating power for their readers as they had for those who first heard them.

The significant quality of these lectures is not that they add to one's store of knowledge but rather that they will lead to an expansion of consciousness, as if windows had been opened in one's mind to see new vistas of truth.

As in climbing a mountain one sees the landscape below from ever changing perspectives, so reading this book will enable one to see life and God and oneself in ever changing light. It may be a deeper understanding or some truth seen with new clarity or an old truth which suddenly flashes with new power.

Certainly this book will be educative in the original sense of drawing from within its readers the truth as they need to see it and as it will have the power to set them free.

Roy McVicar

Contents

of the communities that we create in our world. This is a new humanity from which can spring a new heaven and a new Earth; and those who are the prototypes of the new humanity are those who know that they *are* the New Age and they had better get up and start actualizing it, expressing it, externalizing it, being it.

The life of the Buddha, who is really one of the founders of the New Age consciousness, is called in the East 'the great renunciation.' His life is taken as a parable of the adventure of man's own soul, leaving a high spiritual state in response to the invocation of lesser lives and journeying through three gates—the mind, the emotions and the body—to take up residence in the realms of physical, emotional and mental relativity; and there to become, through having renounced one spiritual level, a great saviour and to gain an even greater spiritual estate.

Buddha is the avatar of wisdom who paves the way for the avatar of love-wisdom who is the Christ. The Christ and his work are related to the New Age, with the true and powerful meaning behind the act of sacrifice. The New Age is not really all that new. It is a continuation of a vast programme of spiritual and evolutionary development initiated ages ago, particularly by the Buddha and the Christ. In their teachings lie all the keys we need to enter the New Age.

One of the reasons that we say we are moving into a new age is because of the cyclic manifestation of energy within nature—not just planetary nature but cosmic nature. For the past twenty-five hundred years the Earth has been largely influenced by a certain quality of energy which is now phasing out and is being replaced by the energy of the Seventh Ray.

It is good in understanding the vision of the New Age to have an understanding of what the Seventh Ray implies and what it is going to create in our world. To have this understanding we need to clarify what is meant by ritual, for the Seventh Ray is occultly known as the ray of ceremonial magic or the ray of ritual.

David Spangler and his vision

David Spangler, age 33, is an American-born writer and educator. In 1964, at the age of 19, while attending Arizona State University and studying biochemistry and genetics, he began lecturing on New Age themes. This developed into a full-time activity and he later introduced and taught an experimental class in esoteric and New Age philosophy for the San Jose Metropolitan Adult Education programme in San Jose, California.

He has held classes and worked with groups in Great Britain and throughout the United States. From 1970 to 1973 he stayed with the Findhorn Community, lecturing and writing and initiating the educational programme which has evolved into the University of Light. Though based now in America, where he is lecturing and teaching, he makes regular visits to Findhorn and is actively involved in the work there.

In June 1970 David Spangler arrived at Findhorn for what was to have been a brief visit, and in fact stayed for three years. During that time he was responsible for setting in motion the educational aspect of Findhorn which transformed from a rapidly expanding community into a University of Light. He gave a tremendous amount of teaching both in the form of lectures which were recorded on tape, and also in the form of books and pamphlets and study papers.

Since much of his teaching, given spontaneously in the spoken word, is both profound and complex, it may be of value to those who study the lectures and those who will read his books, to look at the essence of his thought and clarify the basic truths which he put forward.

At the outset it is necessary to grasp the fact that he did not teach a system of ideas, a structured philosophy which can be set out in a dogmatic form. As those who had the advantage of listening to his lectures are aware, he spoke in the flow of inspiration and not in a carefully thought out pattern.

The result is that his lectures cannot be fully understood just on the intellectual level. They must be listened to, absorbed, and responded to on a deeper level, by the whole man. Because of this there is probably a process of learning in depth which takes place on subconscious levels as one listens to his spoken words, as compared to simply reading his lectures in print.

We may indeed say that David's main purpose in his teaching is not to give us facts and theories, but rather to stimulate our minds and open them to new ideas and to new dimensions of thought. He sets out no cut-and-dried system, but rather aims to awaken our minds and imaginations, and to satisfy the universal need for new levels of awareness, new visions of life. The essential result of hearing and absorbing his teaching is not that we are better informed on any subject though there is a great deal of knowledge included in what he says, but that we are lifted to new and higher levels of consciousness and are able to see and understand and experience life in new ways and with new power and intensity and joy.

What we find then in his educational writings is not truths or ideas which are capable of reasoned and logical proof. They are convincing only because they are true; they find assent because they awaken a chord of recognition in our hearts and minds. As David has said: 'I share the ideas in these lectures as the results of my own experience and as concepts that are meaningful to me. They have no other authority than that. If they are useful to you and serve to open your consciousness to greater levels of life and being, then they have truth for you. If these ideas do not have value for you, then I hope this fact itself will help to clarify where your truth may be found.'

The sincerity and humility of these words run through all his spoken and written teachings.

This is closely related to a further feature of his work, namely that ideas, truths, principles, visions are to be accepted as valid only as and when they are actually demonstrated in practice, and worked out in terms of everyday life, in all the duties, tasks and relationships, that make up the fabric of our lives.

There is everywhere in the world today a deep insistent spiritual hunger which can only be satisfied by a vision that is big enough and deep enough. But such a vision, to win the approval and allegiance of mankind, must have been shown to be practical, through having been lived and proven in action.

Creative solutions to the world's problems will never find acceptance until people have manifested their reality by integrating them into their lives and by proving their effectiveness through concrete demonstration and application to mundane tasks.

Also, such demonstration cannot be effective if it is limited to a few special individuals here and there. Its only effective form of expression will be some community whose aim is to show the validity and reality of living by spiritual laws, and so manifesting a God-inspired individual and community life. Hence the importance of educational centres where such demonstration can take place. David sees the immense value of such places as Findhorn, which provide this essential and universal service through the inspired and dedicated efforts of those who make up the community or who support the Centre in any way.

In the study of any thinker or teacher it is important to isolate what Bergson called his 'central intuition.' This is essential to an understanding of what that thinker has to say. In Teilhard de Chardin this focal point of his thought was evolution, which as he himself said, was not a theory or a hypothesis or a system, but 'a general condition to which all theories, all hypotheses, all systems must bow, and which they must satisfy henceforward if they are to be thinkable and true.' Evolution, he affirmed, 'is a light illuminating all facts, a curve that all lines must follow.'

Can we find, in David's teaching, such a central intuition? In all the complexity of his thinking, amid all the multitude of subjects and themes which throng his lectures, is there a single thread which unites them, an intuition which is 'a light illuminating all facts'?

As I understand him David found this unifying concept in the fact of 'oneness.' This, as he emphasizes, does not mean that everything is the same, but that there is no separation, that everything exists within a unified field of being.

Many aspects of modern development, especially in science, have brought out this basic concept of oneness. For instance, scientific research into nuclear energy has changed the old idea of a solid material universe and revealed that all is a manifestation of energy, and that energy is a unified field or oneness. Again, modern techniques of communication have removed barriers of time and distance, and have brought home to man that we are all living in a single interrelated world in which the divisions of race and nation are unreal. Again ecological research has made vividly clear the interrelated nature of all life upon Earth, including the so-called non-life of the soil and mineral kingdom.

From all directions man is having brought to his awareness the reality of the oneness of all life.

Oneness, David explicity affirms, is a key concept of the New Age and the realization of this fact of oneness is the secret of new age living. In a passage of great strength he states, 'The New Age is fundamentally a change of consciousness from one of isolation and separation to one of communion, attunement and wholeness.' It is this change of consciousness, this realization of oneness which is a vital characteristic of the New Age. It is an awareness which is 'one of keen sensitivity to the needs and direction and development of the whole.' One must realize the oneness, the wholeness of which one is a part and allow that realization to inspire and direct one's life.

Oneness is the key to all the basic concepts in David's teaching, and is the link between the many themes with which he is concerned. It is central to an understanding of what he means by God. In the majority of the great religions, especially in the Judaeo-Christian tradition, it is the transcendence of God which is so often stressed. God is great beyond the power of the human mind to grasp; he is separate in his holiness and majesty, and can be approached only in fear and remorse through special channels of ritual and sacrifice. 'Thus saith the high and lofty one that inhabiteth eternity, whose name is holy.' Small wonder, as David mentioned, that 'in the past man has approached the whole, approached the universal life, God, as if it were a thing apart from him, something in his environment rather than a living presence within himself.'

The New Age must begin from a change in this relationship of man to God, for as man understands his relationship with his Creator, so he shapes his relationships with his fellowmen, with Earth which is his home, and with the cosmos to which he belongs. Through the realization of oneness which is the New Age consciousness, man will come to see that the whole is as much an inner quality as it is a reality outside himself. 'It is only when he realizes that he is one with the whole, that it is indeed his greater self, and that the greatest contribution he can make to it is a joyous blending of his uplifted and Christ-filled personality and being in loving communion and cooperation with the others who share wholeness with him, that he begins to know oneness.'

This redefinition of God will lead further to a new idea and form of communication with him. In so far as he has been thought of as a being outside ourselves, communication such as prayer or meditation or worship was understood as a kind of exchange between man and God, the two being separate; it was contact with a God other than oneself which could be turned on or off according to whether help was needed or not.

When, however, we start from the concept of oneness, prayer can no longer be thought of in terms of an exchange between two separate beings. Communication becomes communion. In David's words: 'The microcosm that we represent within us duplicates in all its aspects the vaster realms of life and consciousness that apparently lie outside and beyond us in the macrocosm. To communicate with a level of life apparently outside us, we simply discover and attune to its corresponding reality within us. We realize that there is no separation, that essentially we are one with that level, and we accept that oneness as the reality.'

For instance, the quality of love within my life is one with love on all levels of its expression throughout the universe. When I love, when I learn to relate to all life around me without fear or hatred or separation, then I become sensitive to the limitless love within all creation. I am not contacting a source of love outside myself; rather I dissolve the barriers between myself and love, I am at one with love.

This New Age concept of prayer, known as attunement, is not just another technique of the inner life. It is a way of life in which we live in the realization of the oneness of all life within us and around us. In times of silence I can increase this awareness so that the whole of my life becomes a more complete attunement to all life on all levels. 'Attunement is walking, working, living every moment in the living presence of God which is oneness.'

From this basic concept of oneness comes also a new and deeper understanding of the nature of man. The age-old question still rises to be answered—what is man? And on the answer to that question depends our understanding of the New Age, and our capacity to be part of it and co-creators of it.

'Man,' wrote David, 'is much, much more than a biological mechanism simply reacting its way through life. Within him flows the creative spirit of life that seeks to go beyond the present form of the world and give birth to new horizons and heights of consciousness. Growth and expansion are the very essence of his spirit and it is nourished by a vision that releases its capacities for growth and gives its life meaning. Man must have a vision of the future that challenges and creatively uplifts him. Without it he loses touch with his greater life and truly sinks to the level of being merely a biological and psychological machine, reacting automatically to the stimuli of life about him.'

Man's true life is to know that he is one with his greater life. In order to know himself, who he is and what he is, he must realize the oneness, the whole of which he is part. He is a divine spirit, at one with God, at one with the creative source. In addition to his physical, emotional and mental natures there is in man that which can say, 'I am,' and even more significantly that which can say, 'I am that I am,' which is the name of divinity.

The true nature of man is fully known in terms of his evolution from being merely a reactor into being a creator. At the beginning man (or what later came to be known as man) was in a state of oneness with God (or what later came to be known as God). He experienced that oneness as naturally and as easily as a fish experiences the ocean.

But to experience is not the same as to participate in, and the destiny of man was to become a participant, a co-creator. Thus from the instinctive life of Nature and his emergence as a part of the natural system of this planet (Birth 1) man moves through his present stage in which he has been developing mind and the sense of individual selfhood (Birth 2) to the breakthrough to his soul consciousness, in which he experiences himself as a creative participant in a universal wholeness and begins to express himself accordingly (Birth 3).

In brief, man has evolved from simply being 'in God' to the level of being that divinity which he inherently is. And the force within creation which has enabled the true nature of man to grow and to change and to unfold is known as the Christ.

In religious thought the Christ is generally identified with his manifestation in the historical Jesus, and his function limited to being the saviour of the world. But the Christ is the ultimate energy moving through creation that is life-giving. He is the educative force within creation, drawing out of matter, out of form, out of experience, out of life, the greater potentials of divinity that are inherent within them.

Further, it is man's destiny to embody the Christ even as Jesus did; for when life knows itself, when it truly knows what it is, then it must identify itself with what it is. It is the Christ nature and realization which it is man's ultimate destiny to experience and to make manifest for the true salvation of his planet.

The Christ manifested as a man to show man his true identity. In essence the Christ message is, 'I am your true self. I am the abundant life that is your true nature. Be what I am. Live my life.'

These and all the other many themes in David's lectures are woven together into an ever-changing pattern of oneness. No article can give adequate expression to the depth, the subtlety and the stimulating vitality of his own words.

Perhaps the best way to draw all the aspects of his teaching together is to quote his account of the aim of education, for this is truly the purpose of his own work: 'We believe that each man must learn to unfold from within himself a deeper awareness of his relationship and responsibility to the wholeness of life. This unfoldment we call true education. It is more than learning certain facts and digesting various traditional opinions. It is learning how to blend one's emotional, mental and spiritual life into wholeness, and to translate this into practical effective service.'

Roy McVicar

Oedipus and Aquarius

What do we mean by the New Age? It can have very concrete meanings, just as sunrise has a very concrete meaning. For many people the concept of the New Age has come into their consciousness because of astrology and modern interest in astrology. This is proclaimed to be the Age of Aquarius. Drama, song and dance serve to present this concept to modern humanity. And it has become something of a catch phrase in many parts of the world to speak about the Age of Aquarius, the children of Aquarius, Aquarian this and Aquarian that.

For other people the concept of the New Age is religiously oriented. It derives from one of the many prophecies that have been made in most of the world's great religions: the return of the Christ, the return of Mohammed, the appearance of the next Buddha, the Maitreya Buddha, the appearance of the next incarnation of Krishna. Most of the great religions carry the concept of the reappearance of, or the remanifestation of a particular prophet, or the light and force behind that prophet, into our age.

In this book we shall discuss some of these prophecies and their symbolic and non-symbolic content, and I particularly want to link the concepts of the New Age with our Christian tradition. This is not to exclude the important material in other religious traditions, that of Buddhism or Hinduism or Islam, but in many ways the force that is working through this

3

Centre, and indeed through many centres that are externalizing the New Age, is a force which in its last great appearance manifested itself as the Christ. In some ways the bridge between Christianity and what it has created in Western culture, the scientific revolution of the past three hundred years and what it has created in the past hundred years, and the concepts of the New Age, all need to be tied together.

We are not going to consider the New Age from a surface point of view, as an event, or indeed as a particular time in human history. What I wish to communicate is what lies behind the concept of the New Age, the timeless reality of the New Age. For the New Age vision is not only applicable now, it has been applicable throughout all of human history. To the extent that we can free our consciousness from being tied to purely time-oriented concepts, to that extent we hold within ourselves the power to experience the New Age now, and to become builders of it and of its external reality. We are interested in consciousness and what moves within consciousness.

I want to begin by going back in time to the writings of Sophocles, the great Attic dramatist and poet. Of all the tragedies of Greek drama, those of Sophocles are perhaps the most compelling in their human essence. All of Greek drama derived from a culture that was very much into the concept of the mysteries, a culture highly attuned to what has come to be known as the esoteric side of life. Those who created the philosophies, the plays and the poems which have come to us from that culture and which form such a large foundation for Western man, were in one way or another directly involved in the initiate mysteries or were influenced by them.

Just as Shakespeare holds multi-levels of meaning and insight into the whole cosmic drama of humanity, the same is true for the ancient Greek plays. One series of plays is called the Theban Trilogy. It is made up of three works of Sophocles: *Oedipus Rex, Oedipus at Colonus,* and *Antigone.* I am particularly interested in sharing with you the story of *Oedipus Rex* and *Oedipus at Colonus.* You will see why this has bearing on the subject of introducing the New Age vision as we go along.

Oedipus is best known to us as the man who had the misfortune of killing his father and marrying the mother. The concept has come down to us in recent years as a description for a particular psychological complex, the Oedipus complex, in which the son is in love with his mother. But Oedipus represents more than simply an individual who was cursed by the Fates to

4

experience and to weave a rather tragic destiny. For those of you who are not familiar with his story, you will be by the time this chapter is finished; and for those of you who are, this will be a refresher course.

Thebes was a Greek city-state. It was being bothered by a unique being called the Sphinx. This being was half woman and half animal. It had a habit of stopping people who were going to and from the city and asking them riddles. If they could answer the riddle, they were free to go; if they could not answer the riddle, they were eaten by the Sphinx. The Sphinx grew very fat because no one could answer her riddles.

One day Oedipus, a traveller, came on the scene and he was stopped by the Sphinx. He was asked a riddle, which he successfully answered. The riddle dealt with the nature of man. In essence it asked, 'What creature is it that begins life on four legs, passes the middle of its life on two legs, and ends up on three legs?', and Oedipus rightly said that it was man: who begins life crawling as a baby, who stands upright on two legs as a man in his prime, but as he gets old and the weight of years begins to drag down his muscles and his legs become weak, he ends up walking with a cane which is the third leg. When the riddle was answered, it destroyed the power of the Sphinx, and the Sphinx was killed.

The people of Thebes were greatly pleased at this. Since their king had disappeared and no one knew what had happened to him, they made Oedipus their king, and gave to him in marriage the widow of the former king. From that marriage there came two sons and two daughters. Oedipus proved himself to be a very wise, a very benevolent and a very just king, and Thebes entered a period of great prosperity. Then all at once it seemed that everything began falling apart, and in the words of the Chorus:

> Earth's blossoms blasted fall,
> Nor can our women rise from childbed after pangs and cries,
> But flocking more and more toward the western shores;
> Soul after soul is known to wing her flight,
> Swifter than quenchless flame,
> Into the far realms of the night.

Crops were failing, animals no longer gave milk, no longer gave young. The women had become barren; those who did give birth, died in childbirth. A great plague had settled upon the city and the surrounding lands. The question was, what had caused this? Obviously some god must be angered. Creon, the brother of the queen, and Oedipus's brother-in-law, was sent to the Oracle at Delphi to inquire of the god Apollo what was amiss. The message came back that the land was stained with blood, that the murderer of the king had not been found and brought to justice, and that until this was done, the curse would be upon Thebes and all her people. Oedipus proclaimed to the people that he would not rest until the murderer had been discovered. He pronounced a curse upon the murderer, saying that no man in Thebes would give him help, or speak to him; he would be an exile driven from the land, and the curses of the gods would rest upon him.

Oedipus sends for the wisest man in the kingdom, who happens to be blind, and asks him to tell him what this man can see of truth. An interesting concept—a blind man, blind from birth, is accounted the greatest seer in the land. But what he tells Oedipus is that *he* is the murderer, and that he is in fact guilty of the crimes of patricide and of incest. Naturally Oedipus thinks the man mad and orders him out of his presence.

But as the play unfolds it becomes apparent that the reason Oedipus came to Thebes was that he was leaving his own country, the city-state of Corinth, where his supposed mother and father dwelt, the king and queen of Corinth. He, too, had gone to Delphi to try and discover just who he was, for he had heard rumours that he was not the natural born son of the king and queen. But the Oracle, instead of telling him of his past, told him that he was destined to kill his father and marry his mother. To keep this from happening, he vowed never to return to his home. He set forth on this journey and came upon a crossroads. A man in a chariot ordered him to stand aside, as he had the right of way, and lashed out at Oedipus with his whip. Oedipus, not being particularly obliged to being whipped that day, lashed out with his staff and killed the man. He then killed all those who were following him, about five in number, only one chancing to escape. It was then that he continued on his journey and met the Sphinx outside the walls of Thebes.

When this accusation is made, it angers Oedipus greatly. However, as the day proceeds, a man appears from Corinth, a shepherd, who announces the fact that the king of Corinth has died and Oedipus is now the king of that city-state if he wishes to return and take up his new crown. But Oedipus says, 'No, I cannot do that, because I'm afraid that even though the king has died, not from my own hands, and the prophecy is therefore obviously false, perhaps it is only half false; and if I go back to Corinth I will end up in some strange way marrying my mother.'

The shepherd informs him that he need not worry about that because the queen really is not his mother; that this shepherd had been given Oedipus as a baby when he was tending flocks on the hillside; that another shepherd in the employ of the king of Thebes had brought him this baby, saying that the queen of Thebes had ordered this baby to be killed, for the Delphic Oracle had prophesied that if she gave birth to a son, the son would end up killing the father. When she gave birth to a son, to keep this from happening she gave the boy to the shepherd and told him to kill him. But the shepherd took pity on this boy and instead gave him to the other shepherd, who took him to Corinth and gave him to the king. The king had no children and decided to raise Oedipus as his own. The name, incidentally, came from the fact that the queen had had the boy's feet pierced and thongs put through them and his feet tied together so that he could not run; Oedipus means 'swollen foot.'

At this time, Oedipus has sent throughout the kingdom for anyone who might have news of the death of the former king, and he tracks down relentlessly this one surviving member of the king's train. It turns out that this was the shepherd to whom he had been given as a baby. It all comes to light that he was indeed the son of the king of Thebes, that it was he who killed the king, and had returned to marry his mother. So the prophecies had been fulfilled.

Oedipus cries out. Having discovered this horrible fact, the queen rushes out and kills herself. Oedipus blinds himself, tearing out his eyes. He says:

My curse on him who from the cruel bond
That held my feet in that high pasture land
Freed me and rescued me from murder there,
And saved my life.
Vain kindness! Then to have died
Had spared this agony to me and mine;
Then had I ne'er been proved a patricide,
Ne'er borne the shame of marriage bonds incestuous;
But now I am god-abandoned, son of the unholy,
Rival of him who gave me being.

The play ends with Oedipus being led, blinded, back into the palace to be kept there until Creon, acting as regent, could decide what to do with him.

Oedipus at Colonus was written much later in Sophocles' life. It carries on the story of what happens to Oedipus as an old man, and from our point of view represents the most important part of the Trilogy.

Oedipus was kept in the palace at Thebes until his eldest son became king, and banished him from the kingdom. Blinded, he was led from town to town and from village to village by his two daughters, one in particular, Antigone, until finally, a very old man, he arrives at a sacred grove outside Athens, in a small suburb called Colonus. Through some inner knowing he realizes that this grove has been his destiny all his life, that this is where the Fates have led him.

The Oedipus that we meet in this play is quite different from the first Oedipus, who was a man very noble, very much a kind and wise king, but cursed by this fate. The Oedipus in this second play begins as a rather querulous old man, who has suffered a great deal but who has learned through this suffering a great patience where life is concerned. The bulk of the play concerns the efforts that he has to make to fulfil the final prophecies made by the Oracle at Delphi, and to avoid being used as a pawn in a power struggle that is occurring at Thebes.

His youngest son has led a coup d'etat and ousted the older brother, who in turn goes to another city and marries the richest girl there, raises an army and returns to lay siege to Thebes in order to regain his throne. The Oracle at Delphi says that whoever can claim the body of Oedipus, alive or dead, will win this battle. But the Oracle also says that should Oedipus die in a foreign land, then Thebes will be cursed and will fall; and whichever city does receive Oedipus will be blessed and will rise to new heights. The king of Athens is Theseus, and more about that in a moment.

When Oedipus arrives at this grove, he is blind. He does not know it is a sacred grove, except that he feels a presence there that impels him into it. He sits down. A number of the town folk come up and tell him he has to leave; it is a grove in which no human being is supposed to be. And when they discover who he is then they really do want him to go, for they are afraid that the curse that has followed him throughout his life will descend on them. But Antigone pleads with them, and Oedipus says that he is now a messenger of the gods, not the bearer of a curse. In the end Theseus comes to see him. Theseus recognizes that Oedipus is now the bearer of some strange spiritual force; that though he is blind, he has developed a strange new sight and is himself possessed by the spirit of the gods.

Both Creon from Thebes, and Polynices the older brother from Argos arrive, each one trying to claim Oedipus. Creon goes so far as to take his daughters prisoner. But Theseus rescues them. Oedipus curses both Creon and his oldest son and sends them away. For those who are interested, the third play in the Trilogy, *Antigone,* describes what happens to them. They all end up being killed outside the walls of Thebes. But Oedipus is left in this sacred grove, and what happens to him is most interesting.

It is the end of the play, and Theseus has protected Oedipus; he has put the power of Athens at his disposal, and now Oedipus is going to pay back this debt. He intends, then, to proclaim a great blessing upon the city, and he says to Theseus:

> I will instruct thee now in rites
> That shall remain an ageless treasure
> To thy countrymen.
> I will presently, with no man guiding me,
> Conduct thee to the spot where I must die.
> This is thy secret not to be revealed
> To any one of men,
> Or where 'tis hid, or whereabout it lies;
> 'Tis for thee to keep invoilate while thou livest,
> And when thy days are ending,
> Breathe it to the foremost man,
> And he alone in turn unto the next successively.
> So shalt thou ever hold Athens
> Unravished by the dragon brood.

(This is a reference to the soldiers of Thebes.)

> Cities are numberless, and anyone may likely insult
> Even those who dwell secure;
> For the eye of heaven, though late,
> Yet surely sees, when casting off respect,
> Men turn to crime.
> Let that be far from thee;
> A warning needless to a man so wise.
>
> Now we go, for this leading of the gods is urgent,
> To the place nor loiter more;
> This way, my children, follow me,
> For I am now thy guide as ye were mine;
> Nay, touch me not, but leave me of myself
> To find the holy sepulchre
> Wherein this form must rest beneath Athenian soil.

The two dauthers and Theseus follow Oedipus, who though blind can now see, deep into the depths of this grove. Later a Messenger comes back—a

Messenger is a convenient device used in Greek plays to help the story along—
and says to the Chorus:

> Athenian citizens, my briefest tale were to say singly,
> Oedipus is gone;
> But to describe the scene enacted yonder
> Craves no brief speech, nor was the action brief.

Chorus: Then he is gone? Poor man!

Messenger: Know it once for all,
He hath left eternally the light of day.

Chorus: Poor soul! What, ended he with peace divine?

Messenger: Aye, there is the main marvel;
How he moved from hence thou knowest,
For thou too were here,
And saw that of his friends none guided him;
But he they loved was leader to them all.

> Now when he came to the steep pavement
> Rooted with adamant foundations deep in earth,
> On one of the many paths he took his stand,
> Near the stone basin.
> There opposite the mass of laurean ore,
> Turned from the Hollow-Pear-Tree and the Tomb of Marble,
> He sat down and straight undid his travel-soiled attire;
> Then called aloud on both his children,
> And bade someone fetch pure water
> From a running stream.

(And Oedipus undergoes a rite of cleansing.)

> When he was satisfied and nothing now remained undone
> Of all he bade them do,
> The god of Darkness thundered;
> And the maids stood horror-stricken on hearing,
> Then together fell at their father's knees and wept
> And wailed loudly and long,
> With beating of the breast.

> He, when that sound of sorrow pierced his ear,
> Caressed them in his arms and said,
> 'My daughters, from this day forth
> You have no more father.
> All that was mine is ended,
> And no longer shall ye continue
> Your hard ministry of labour for my life,

And yet, though hard, not unendurable,
Since all the toil
Was rendered light through love.'

Such was the talk, mingled with sobs and crying,
As each clung fast to each;
But when they came to an end of weeping,
And these sounds were stilled,
First, all was silent,
Then a sudden voice hurried him onward,
Making each man's hair bristle on end
With force of instant fear;
Now here, now there, not once
But often times a god called loudly:
'Oedipus, Oedipus, why thus delay our going?
This long while we are stayed for,
And thou tarriest. Come away.'

He, when he knew the summons of the gods,
Gave word for royal Theseus to go near;
And when he came, said:
'Friend forever kind, reach thy right hand,
I pray thee, to these my children;
Daughters, yours to him, and give thy sacred word
That thou wilt never betray these willingly,
But still perform all that thou mayest
With true thought for their good.'

(Echoes of another being who said, 'John, behold your mother. Mother,
behold your son.')

Theseus, with great calmness like his noble self, promised on oath to
keep this friendly bond. When he had done so, Oedipus forthwith, stroking
his children with his helpless hands, spake thus:

'My daughters, you must steel your hearts
To noble firmness, and depart from hence,
Nor ask to see or hear forbidden things.
Go at once. Theseus alone must stay,
Sole rightful witness of these mysteries.'

These accents were the last we all might hear;
Then following the two maids with checkless tears and groans,
We took our way;
But by and by, at a distance looking round,
We saw, not him,.who was not there,

But Theseus all alone,
Holding his hand before his eyes
As if some apparition, light unendurable,
Had dazed his vision.

By what fate Oedipus perished,
Mortal man, save Theseus, cannot say.
The lower part of earth perhaps,
Where comes no pain,
Opened kindly to receive him in,
Not bemourned nor with a tearful end of sickness
Was he taken from the earth;
But wondrously beyond recorded fate.

And at the end, Theseus says to the daughters who are still weeping:
'Come, lament no more;
His destiny has found its perfect end.'

Oedipus is an initiate heroic figure. Theseus is the same, but there is a subtle difference between the two. In these two plays, for those who held the key to the historic symbolism involved, a great cosmic drama was unfolded concerning the nature and destiny of man. What other being, in a cosmic sense, could be said to have killed his father and married his mother?

The answer to that riddle, like the answer that Oedipus gave to the Sphinx, is man. The destiny of man has been, through mind, to slay the link he knew with his father source; and taking to himself certain creative powers to blend with his mother, or nature, or the creative primal laws, from which he sought to create his world.

Oedipus represents most clearly that level of consciousness through which man has passed, that is the mind. Notice how Oedipus gained his power. It was through answering the riddle of the Sphinx. The Sphinx, long used as symbol of the world and its hidden nature; and the mind of man, the analytical mind, the probing mind, the mind that riddles the mysteries of nature and seeks the answers to those riddles, has been a stage through which man has passed. In so doing man has, of necessity in some cases, of unwitting destiny in others, placed himself often outside the sphere of attunement to his source. The mind is like that. The mind that can seek to answer the riddles of the universe is a mind that will turn away from that which cannot be answered by its devices.

Early scientists were most religious men, but set forth the initial pattern that the ultimate questions and mysteries of life had no place in science, for science could deal only with that which could be open to demonstrable proof, or the absence of demonstrable proof. For the scientific method is not an approach towards truth, as much as it is an approach to determining what is not true, what is false under the facts of empirical investigation.

Thebes—though undoubtedly this would not have been present as a concept that long ago—is very much the equivalent of what Teilhard de Chardin calls the 'noosphere,' that realm that is the product of man's mental consciousness, of man's creative thought. Man has taken unto himself the powers of the gods, without knowing his godliness. Like the ancient Thebes we too begin to suffer the consequences: a polluted Earth, a world in which the products of the mind have outstripped the products of the heart, or in which the heart has been used to create separation and not unity.

In short, man has suffered blindness, and like Oedipus, has moved out of his father's house into a long pilgrimage upon the Earth, in which though he has been able to see in physical senses he has remained blind to the reality of the world and the reality of himself.

Oedipus is not a tragic figure. He is an heroic figure in that his destiny is perfect. He is caught up not in death but in translation. In the end, though blind, it is he who sees and leads the others. Antigone and Ismene, his two daughters—who represent the products of the human mind; knowledge and invention are not evil of themselves by any means, but are able—if man will let them—to lead him to his destiny, though unable to participate in that destiny themselves. Man's computers, for example, can lead him into greater knowledge and his mind becomes transcendent. His computers cannot share in that transcendency. They cannot enter the sacred grove of man's destiny, though they may help him attain it.

Oedipus is man, blinded because he has expressed his creative powers not in unity with the source but as a separate being, and in that sense lying incestuously with the nature that gives him birth. Oedipus also represents the destiny of man transfigured into light, and through the darkness of blindness gaining a vision transcendent greater than those who have not had that vision.

Yet one being, one mortal, was able to share the destiny of Oedipus and witness what transpired for him. That was Theseus. This is very interesting because Theseus became king of Athens through a similar heroic action. Oedipus was hero because he solved a riddle. He was hero because of his mind; he reached the heights and then fell, for his mind had an integrity and nobility that would not allow it to rest with anything less than the truth. The compelling tragedy of *Oedipus Rex* is that even though the audience begins to know quite clearly what is happening and at every step along the way Oedipus is told by the wise men, and by the queen to stop looking. 'Stop looking! If you keep investigating then sorrow will be upon you.' But Oedipus would say, 'No matter what the price, I must know the truth. I will know who I am.'

But Theseus is a different figure. He too is an initiate. He is the one who sailed with the captive maidens and young men to Crete, at that time a powerful nation which held the city-state of Athens under its thumb and demanded tribute—the tribute being young virgin lives to be sacrificed to the Minotaur in the Labyrinth. Theseus is the one who entered the Labyrinth, winding his thread behind him as he went, faced the Minotaur and destroyed it; then following the thread led himself and those who had been chosen as the sacrificial victims back into the light.

This drama has also been used to portray the destiny of man, the nature of man, but a different nature than that of Oedipus. Here is the being who descends into the maze of human emotion, wherein the virgin powers of the soul are sacrificed—the maze of separateness, the maze of thought and feeling so intermixed that one cannot distinguish between them; until there is encountered the destroyer, the beast man, the man that has not yet risen above the animal level, the instinctual man, the reactive consciousness, the lower consciousness. Theseus, guided and protected by the thread to the realms of light, destroys this lower self and emerges the initiate being—the lower self overcome, the beastly part of man destroyed, and the king born. Theseus returns to Athens, the power of Crete having been destroyed, and is made the king.

Two kings meet in this sacred grove; one an initiate who has moved through darkness and has learned light through darkness, the initiate of the mind; and the other the initiate of the soul who also entered the darkness of the labyrinth but emerged triumphant. Because symbolically he had proved himself master of himself, a transfigured being through his own efforts, he was allowed to watch the transfiguration of Oedipus. Oedipus was not transfigured through his own efforts. His transfiguration came through the product of fate. It was not through his doing; in fact he makes a great point of this in *Oedipus at Colonus*, telling everyone who will listen to him that it was not his fault that he killed his father and married his mother, it was just that his father and mother must have done something pretty bad that he was sent as their punishment. Therefore no one should blame him because, after all, the Fates had made him what he was. He ends up a transfigured being through the suffering of his soul.

What does this have to do with the Aquarian Age? We now arrive at the point where mankind stands in the sacred grove. Man as a whole is moving as Oedipus moved, seemingly a victim of fate, towards a destiny of light, but moving in blindness—man who has in many ways killed his consciousness of his father, or of his source, or of his divinity, and has made himself, in the words of the dramatist, the rival of his source and by so doing has taken the creative powers to be his bride, creating as he wants to create and not necessarily as harmony and balance would have things created. But through this man is learning, as Oedipus learned.

Now at this time man comes out of the realms of Thebes, the lower mind, to the realms of Athens, the higher mind and the spirit—Athens, the centre of one of the greatest inspirational outpourings the world has known, where for a brief hundred years a light shone in human culture that rivals anything the planet has seen; Athens, the home of the initiate consciousness. In Athens the king is Theseus, the man who has faced himself in the labyrinth of his being, has not waited upon fate but has gone in plunging into the darkness, unravelling behind him the thread of his faith and his courage and his attunement; and there has faced what he is and has known that that is not what he is at all, and emerges with the thought-form destroyed, a past redeemed, and a crown upon his head—the initiate consciousness and the human consciousness moving together for a destiny.

Where do we stand at this point? We have the choice as human beings of continuing along the path of Oedipus, maintaining our blindness, yet knowing that out of darkness will come light. Or we have the choice of calling in upon ourselves the power of our higher nature, entering the labyrinth of our being and emerging therefrom, the Christed soul. Both gain self-knowledge, but gain it in different ways and providing different powers.

In this sacred grove of time, the gods are calling, 'Man, man! We have tarried long and await your coming.'

Theseus, the Christ, the illumined mind, is there to guide humanity to answer that call with vision, that man does not walk in darkness but possesses within himself that inner light which can show the way more clearly than

15

anything else, than any physical sight certainly, or sight of mind; that through mind, emotion and physical effort the new is not created, but another force is needed—a force that can be bestowed upon man if man waits long enough, but which man can invoke for himself through his own courageous efforts.

The New Age is a point of time when new energies pour forth upon the Earth to increase and to heighten man's awareness. It is also an intimate and individual point of timeless realization when we see that whatever our past, whatever our fates, whatever our nature has been, none of these things are what we are. What we are cannot truly be described by mortal man, nor mortal mind; but what we are is that which transpires when light reaches down to light, and the individual is transfigured, taken into a different realm beyond the sight of man. So many prophecies now speak of this, of people being moved in the twinkling of an eye into a different realm. That realm is within us, and our translation into it is a matter of consciousness and of attitude.

We shall explore this in greater detail and see how, by releasing the powers of Theseus so to speak, we can bring the Oedipus-like nature of man to the point of its perfect destiny; and at that point know that we are the New Age, that it lives within us and awaits its birth.

CHAPTER
TWO

Four Horsemen of Aquarius

I want to begin with a passage from *The New English Bible—New Testament,* Book of Revelation, Chapter 6, Verses 1 to 8. The vision that Saint John has been having has described the beings that have appeared before him bearing with them seven seals:

> Then I watched as the Lamb broke the first of the seven seals; and I heard one of the four living creatures say in a voice like thunder, 'Come!' And there before my eyes was a white horse, and its rider held a bow. He was given a crown, and he rode forth, conquering and to conquer.
>
> When the Lamb broke the second seal, I heard the second creature say, 'Come!' And out came another horse, all red. To its rider was given power to take peace from the earth and make men slaughter one another; and he was given a great sword.
>
> When he broke the third seal, I heard the third creature say, 'Come!' And there, as I looked, was a black horse; and its rider held in his hand a pair of scales. And I heard what sounded like a voice from the midst of the living creatures, which said, 'A whole day's wage for a quart of flour, a whole day's wage for three quarts of barley-meal! But spare the olive and the vine.'

> When he broke the fourth seal, I heard the voice of
> the fourth creature say, 'Come!' And there, as I
> looked, was another horse, sickly pale; and its rider's
> name was Death, and Hades came close behind. To
> him was given power over a quarter of the earth, with
> the right to kill by sword and by famine, by pestilence
> and wild beasts.

In this passage John is describing what has come to be known as the 'four horsemen of the Apocalypse': conquest, war, famine and death. Down through the centuries since this revelation was given writers and artists have found the theme of 'the four horsemen' a very tantalizing and provocative one.

Many people feel that the revelation of John deals with the age in which we are now moving, and as a consequence there is a certain fear that in our time the four horsemen will be unleashed. It goes without saying that in history these four horsemen have already ridden forth upon the Earth. Certainly the Second World War was an example of this. But there are four other horsemen who, in their riding out upon the planes of human consciousness, are having the greatest effect upon our lives and being in this time.

The New Age vision can be described through the imagery of these four horsemen: four qualities of consciousness which are affecting us now. In the last chapter we looked at Oedipus as man who creates his world through his mind, but through that creation and the invoking of certain powers, without full realization and understanding of those powers, sows the seeds of destruction. We also spoke of Theseus, the initiate king who represents the man who enters into the labyrinth of his own being, there comes face to face with his lower nature and transmutes it, and thereby becomes the new king. We shall call upon those images, as well, in this chapter.

What are the four horsemen of Aquarius? The first horseman we may call, 'the horseman of illusion and of unassimilated works and energy.' When this world was created the planes or realms of thought and feeling were as pure as any unwritten slate may be. Through man's growth he has projected into these realms; he has manipulated through his own feeling and mental natures the energies of these realms, and has created therein various qualities which we call thought-forms.

A thought-form is a complex of energy which has been drawn together about a seed point, the seed point being an image of thought in which it takes on the quality of feeling which is associated with that thought. A thought-form is like a robot. It is created; it is artificial, and it can only do what it is programmed to do. It will keep doing that thing until it runs out of energy or is in some way dispersed. Man has created many of these thought-forms. They are not visible except to those who are clairvoyant. But they have been seen, and can be seen, by highly sensitive people.

The four horsemen of the Apocalypse are such thought-forms which are built up by large numbers of people—whole nations or races tend to take on definite archetypal qualities. They take on universal qualities. They are not specifically related to any one person but affect all the people who are within that particular race or nation or group. Many thought-forms of this nature have been created in the past. In so doing, man has created something else. Teilhard de Chardin speaks of the creation of the noosphere, which is literally the realm which is built up of everything that man has thought or felt—all his inventions, all his ideas, all his books, all his cities. Everything that he has built, everything that does not evolve naturally from the biosphere, the natural world, but which evolves because of man's efforts is contained within the noosphere.

In similar fashion man has created the astral plane. The astral plane really has no existence. It has come into existence because of qualities of energy which man has released and projected from himself as being extensions of himself—in other words, illusions. For example: I look upon an event; I see therein not what is actually occurring, but what I think is occurring, what I would like to occur, what my reactions to this event may be. This is a well-known phenomenon amply demonstrated in psychology classes in which events are staged for the class, and then they are asked to describe what has taken place. The class is unable to do so; that is, the descriptions in no way tally with the event itself.

Such projections from within an individual, which does not reflect clearly the reality of a given situation, nevertheless has existence; and its existence, its particular energy-form, cumulatively throughout the centuries within the massed thought of humanity, has come to form what we now call the astral plane. One of the reasons why it is suggested that people who are on the initiate path do not deal with the astral plane is because, in point of fact, it does not exist. In order to deal with it, you have to acknowledge its existence in such a way that you become yourself captive of it.

The great initiates do deal with this plane, but they deal with it obliquely. I can give you a mythological legend that reflects this. No man could look upon the gorgon without being turned to stone. Perseus, who slew the gorgon, did so by gazing upon a mirror in which this woman with the serpentine hair was reflected; in true marksman style, he slashed his sword while gazing through this mirror and lopped off her head.

The astral plane is very much that way. The being who confronts it directly is turned into the matter of that plane; the being who confronts it obliquely from a mental level, from a higher level, is able to deal with it. The astral plane itself is the plane of illusion.

I am not speaking of a place which deals with emotional energy except in so far as emotion itself is the source of illusion. Emotion, the twin of intuition, is unfortunately the distorted twin. Intuition sees and knows clearly what is, but not in a separate way. It is the essence of empathy, the true source of compassion and emotion. Emotion sees not what is but the reactions to what is one's own internal state, and projects it.

The horseman of illusion, then, comprises the astral plane and all the thought-forms which dwell there. Another way of saying this is that present man is surrounded with an excess of baggage which has no relevancy whatsoever to anything that he is doing or thinking or attempting to do. It is purely the product of the past, yet it is highly active and continues to condition man in various ways. This plane, until such time as the human race itself finally meets the test of it and dispels it, will remain as one of the great testers of humanity. It provides the test of discrimination, the test between emotion and intuition.

An example of how this affects us at this time is the existence on the astral plane of a very powerful thought-form born out of an event held within the racial memory of the Aryan race, which is the progenitor of the source of Western culture as we know it,—a thought-form that can best be expressed by the simple phrase, 'original sin,' the Fall, a concept which has no meaning whatsoever to the root races, the oriental races, that have preceded our own. Part of the reason for this is that the Aryan race is the first race in evolutionary progression of man to come into full grips with the power of mind. Perhaps I should say here that what I mean by the Aryan race is not the blond, blue-eyed superman that Hitler was speaking of, or the Germanic race. The Aryan race is a generic term that refers to that group of people which migrated millennia ago from Asia, and spread throughout Africa and Europe.

This is the first race that has dealt with the problem of mind; and in the great Vedic teachings, which are the first sacred writings of the Aryan race and became the source of Hinduism, the mind is called, 'the slayer of the real.' The mind as we have been moving through it—not necessarily the mind in its totality but the mind as we have been using it—pulls down, encases spirit into form, and then chops it up into little pieces, hoping that by analyzing these little pieces it will come to understand the form; and by understanding the form, it will come to understand the spirit. The mind used in this way becomes the great discriminator, but at the same time it becomes the great judge; that is, it postulates the conditions under which it will discriminate. This means—to use biblical analogy—that it must eat of 'the fruit of the tree of the knowledge of good and evil.'

The use of this mental energy did precipitate a form of fall for man, certainly Western man; and interestingly enough in its initial stages, as the last remnants of the root race, the Atlantean race, attempted to capture this pattern of mind and to use it, it brought about the downfall of that race, the downfall of that culture and that continent. For mind, primitive mind, coupled with the incredible psychic powers of that race, opened the first doors upon the planet to the ingress of what has come to be called the forces of evil.

Existing in the thought patterns of the world today, the astral realm, are still the cumulative effects of that racial memory of the fall, racial memory of the destruction of Atlantis, racial memory of a certain shadow that pursues humanity. There is a book circulating in the Community called, *The Wizard of Earthsea*. This book is highly significant in that it portrays in fantasy form the story of a young boy who goes to a school of magicians and learns to be a wizard. He is actually one of the best wizards in this whole culture. He is a natural born wizard, so much so that he can invoke powers that no other wizard can invoke. In a fit of competition he does invoke a power through his native ability, but without wisdom, without training. He invokes a power from the dark realms which becomes his shadow and seeks to destroy him.

The essence of the book is how he has eventually to confront the shadow of his own creation because it pursues him throughout this realm. He cannot escape it; he must confront it and in some way close the door from which it came. In the great invocation that was given to the world by the Hierarchy a number of years ago, there is a line that says, 'to seal the door

23

where evil dwells.'

In the consciousness of man, then, there exists this image of the shadow and of what man must go through to purge himself of this shadow. Much of the imagery that has become associated with this, with the concept of the fall and with the introduction of sin into the world, is the kind of guilty thought pattern that is self-destructive. 'If I can only suffer enough, I will in some way purge this shadow from the land.'

To me, this is the most powerful and the most menacing of the great ancient thought-forms that remain within the astral plane and are confronting man as he moves into the New Age.

What does this have to do with the New Age? It means that we are now at a time in the development of our culture when we are on a higher level of the spiral than that reached by the Atlantean race. We are ready to send forth into the world what will in future days become known as the sixth root race, the race that masters intuition, as our race, the fifth, is seeking to master the mind. We are at a point very similar to that reached by the Atlantean culture though utilizing different energies; what we now have in atomic power, they had in an incredible form of a psychic power far beyond anything that we know of today. Thank heavens! And as a consequence, this memory looms over the race, of forthcoming destruction. In some way man is again going to teeter on the brink, almost like a lemming, desiring to invoke fire and doom upon himself in order to purge himself of this shadow.

When I lived in California, it was an interesting experience rising into the planes of higher consciousness and having to move through a belt that encompassed the whole State. This belt, when passing through it, contained the most incredible image of the destruction of the State. They were right there: San Francisco crumbling into the sea, and Los Angeles disappearing in a cloud of smoke, and so on. Once more these images were influencing consciousness, weighing on consciousness, creating fear; but more than fear, creating an impulse towards the creation of that very image. An image, a thought-form, is a living being, after a manner of speaking. It will seek form, it will seek reality, it will seek externalization.

Rising above that barrier I found an entirely different set of images in which none of these things took place, but in which California, with minor earth changes here and there as part of the natural evolution of the planetary crust, was becoming a centre, a powerful centre for the revelation of new light and new understanding of the divine will. Two images entirely opposed to each other in many respects.

So the first horseman that goes out is a very ancient being, the horseman of illusion, the thought-forms of the past which seek to make themselves real in our generation, which through every channel that human mind and emotion can provide will seek to externalize themselves, and in some way attempt to expiate, to cleanse what is considered to be an ancient sin, an ancient guilt, an ancient shadow.

The second horseman is the horseman of evolution, of progress. This horseman represents the natural energies of continuous growth following on from the impulses that we have already anchored. When we say we are moving into a new age, the people who attune to the first horseman perceive in consciousness a period of great destruction and cataclysmic change, a vast cleansing. In other words, the emphasis here is on cleansing, but cleansing with a vengeance, cleansing in the sense of crucifixion, cleansing in the sense of sins being washed away through blood.

Then the chosen ones, the elite, those who in some way believe or in some way change themselves, whatever the metaphysical dogma of a particular group may be, will emerge into a new age where—and I quote some things I have been told from leaders of groups—all will wear robes and we will know all things; there will be no sorrow, there will be no disease, there will be no necessity to work. We will simply think and everything is there before us, and we will be as wise as the gods—the modern equivalent of an ancient fairy tale.

Those who follow the second horseman see the New Age emerging in a different fashion, as expressed by a recent book that has come out in America called *Future Shock*, by Alvin Toffler. In this book, this man who is a futurist is projecting and extrapolating from modern technological trends into what the future is going to hold. Obviously we are definitely on the brink of a new age. Not only on the brink, we have actually toppled over!

With the development in nuclear technology, all the developments in the pure sciences, in genetics, in molecular biology, in the ability which is now coming ever closer to hand through genetic surgery to manipulate and determine the exact qualities of offspring, through computer science and the development of third, fourth and fifth generation computers, each one of which multiplies by several factors the capacity of the earlier generation because the computers are designing themselves, through enhanced communication, through space technology, through all of these things that science has brought—and science is the direct manifestation of the fifth root race attempt to master mind and to use the energies of mind—a new age is upon us. We have a technology. We have an energy. We have capabilities at our disposal to completely remake this world.

If the first horseman has his way, this technology will destroy us; but the second horseman is simply the logical progression of growth which is bringing to us constantly an acceleration of our knowledge of the physical universe, and our ability to manipulate that universe and to change it. There is no doubt this is creating a new age. It is one of the prime moving factors behind the changes of consciousness, the pressures upon consciousness, now occurring. Man is stepping into a world altered by his science that is as unlike the world in which he has grown up as the Earth is unlike the Moon.

The third horseman I could call, 'the rider of the purple sage,' for his symbol is purple. He is the horseman of Aquarius and represents, not the progressive energies of the old patterns which are still good patterns, but new energies, the energies of Aquarius, the energies of the Seventh Ray. Here we have impulses designed to bring people together in groups, small and large groups, and to enhance their ability to function together so that they work, not as individuals but the group is able to function as a totally integrated and organic unit.

For this to happen the communion of close communication is required. So the Seventh Ray is, par excellence, the ray of communication, for you cannot have ordered activity without communication. The impact of this energy upon human consciousness is to break down all barriers that prohibit communication, and to train individuals in establishing those bridges that enhance it. When this energy plays upon the energies of developing science, it leads to the kind of developments that we have: enhanced transportation, air travel, rail travel, roads, ships; and enhanced communications technology, telephone, telegraph, satellite communication, television, microwave and eventually telepathy.

The impact of the Seventh Ray tends to break down forms which have stood by themselves so that the energy within those forms can learn how to blend with other energies and other forms into greater and more complex units. It also tends to work on an individual to try and break down individual tendencies towards isolation and separativeness. This energy is symbolized by the zodiacal image of Aquarius, the outpouring of new life upon the Earth, vitalization upon the Earth; and it is a time-controlled thing, a cyclic manifestation. The Seventh Ray is coming into prominence now. It began coming in about five hundred years ago, and it will not reach its peak for another thousand or so years. But it is definitely coming into prominence. It will come into prominence and then will fade out.

This means that, just like in Jesus' time when a Sixth Ray was coming in, we are now at a time when a new dispensation is upon us. We have the concept of the new, that which has not been revealed before. This is really where the whole idea of the New Age has come from, in a spiritual sense: the coming in of new energies, the revelation of new wisdom, new teaching, new understanding, new insight.

These three horsemen—illusion, evolution and Aquarius—all have one thing in common: they ride the 'steeds of time.' They are all in some way time oriented. They are either the rotting phantoms of the past which yet exercise their fascination over modern consciousness, or they are the manifestation of what could be called 'Father Time,' the chain of cause and effect, one thing leading inexorably to another. They are the presence of a new being who is coming to the Earth for the first time, a being who is not a man or a woman but is symbolically a whole personification of new life, new energy and new vision. But all of these are related to time.

The fourth horseman could be called the horseman of infinity, of eternity, of the Christ. There is no bearing on time whatsoever, and yet it is the true essence and meaning of the New Age. When man was created he was created to fulfil a divine plan. A more accurate way of saying that is to say: God exists, and within his being a dream exists, and man is an aspect of God taking a certain kind of form to fulfil that dream. Man is like the Word, he is like the Christ, he was with the Father before time. There is no beginning to what man is; there is no end to what man is—and I speak now of man, not in his form but in his spirit, in his essence.

In that centre of man the New Age has always been, and ages yet to come, and ages that have already cast their treasures upon the Earth and have retired. Within man is this timeless quality, a quality of stillness, of silence, of beingness, which is infinite in its power. It is this divine centre that man is seeking to tap and to externalize. And the whole cosmic drama of humanity is simply the condensation into a time environment of the outgrowth of this divine manifestation.

What is a tree? Is a tree the seed? Is it the sapling? Is it the full grown plant? Is it the new seed? No. A tree is an idea that is living and expresses itself through many forms. We see these forms in a sequence that we call growth, and yet the idea of tree does not grow. It only appears to grow. The tree has been there in its fullness all the time. Man is here now in his fullness. Throughout the ages and whatever kind of dispensation man has been given, there have been many individuals who have realized this. They have gone beyond the limitations of their culture and time, have touched their divine centre and have entered into timelessness. Of these beings those who have chosen to remain behind, to continue working with the evolution of Earth, we call the masters, the initiates, the adepts.

Let us not forget, when we see passing before us the three horsemen of Aquarius who ride the 'steeds of time,' that all of their work and all of their pressure is simply designed to enable us to realize our timelessness. The true New Age vision is not anything that can be related in terms of what is happening now that is different from what was happening a hundred years ago, a thousand years ago, or a thousand years in the future. If we see the New Age in those terms we will experience a certain kind of manifestation, but we may not touch the centre where our true freedom and our true power lies.

Oedipus, the mind of man, Aryan man, accomplished certain things, and the kingdom of Thebes prospered. The mind represented by Oedipus destroyed the Sphinx, the mystery that bred fear and superstition and death. The mind is still doing that in many ways. But Oedipus is best remembered for killing his father and marrying his mother; which is symbolically stating that you cut yourself off from the source, and you then use your own personal power to blend with the creative forces that God has given to create form. These forms may be highly advantageous, they may be very beautiful, but they are incomplete. They hold within them the seeds of blindness and Oedipus did become blind. Yet through his blindness he eventually discovered light and was translated in the sacred grove at Colonus.

This is the drama of modern man. We are beginning to perceive as a race that there really is something more we have to deal with than the pure scientific method, the pure mental approach or the pure emotional approach. All of these are to some extent of the past, although they have some way yet to go in the future before they reach their full peak.

The development of man now reaches a point where he begins to realize certain bindnesses, and sets forth as Oedipus set forth, led by his daughter, the products of his creativity, to try and find the truth, to try and find greater awareness, greater understanding. This whole thing involves the three horsemen: the first horseman which could be called the Fates which will have their will as long as man surrenders himself to the power of time; the second horseman is the journey, the natural outgrowth of man's continuing experience; and the third horseman is the bringing of man to yet another step in his evolution that will show him a little bit more of the universe, and begin to unveil a little greater power than he has had before, a little greater insight.

But it is still only a step. The Seventh Ray is just a step. It is not the wholeness. It is not the end. It is not the best of all possible rays. It is nothing more than just what it is: the introduction of a certain kind of point of view which man must now cultivate, and a certain kind of directive action which man must now obey and follow through on and give embodiment to. Theseus, who enters the labyrinth, discovers the centre of his being and slays therein the creations of his past, the Minotaur, goes directly to the fourth horseman, the timeless state, the divine state, the state that is no more encapsulated within the New Age than it is encapsulated within any age. That being becomes the true initiate who can then help Oedipus to his end. It is Theseus who protects Oedipus and enables him to achieve his translation.

What I wish to portray here is an understanding of the New Age in its *time* aspect, but much more importantly an understanding of our potential as *timeless* beings, because man is going to enter a new age whether he likes it or not. He cannot help it. The forces are there and moving, and man will simply go along with it. It will either be a pleasant ride or it will be a rocky one. Those people who can really grasp the vision, not of the New Age but of themselves and of the centre that is within and can begin to externalize that, have the power to truly direct and enlighten man's transition into Aquarius, man's movement through time, the timeless shepherd that guides the flocks through time.

All of us, then, feel this pressure, the pressure of the four horsemen of Aquarius: pressure of the past, pressure of modern society and its institutions and their development, pressure of the new energies, and the pressure of our soul which demands that we take again the opportunity that Jesus offered, that Buddha offered, that Mohammed offered, that Plotinus offered, that Pythagoras offered, that all the great initiates have offered; that in this moment when things are in such ferment and such vitality and such energy, we step out of time into timelessness, out of form into formlessness, out of one identity into the God-identity. That pressure of the soul is upon us.

The four horsemen of Aquarius: if we deal with them creatively, we shall close the stables for the four horsemen of the Apocalypse. If we miss the vision, then perhaps the four horsemen of Aquarius will be followed by the other four. It is really up to us. The great test is once again upon humanity. We must be very careful of the insights, the concepts, the archetypes, the images we use to describe it; for if we are not careful we will step into a new age of form but miss the opportunity of stepping into the freedom of timelessness. We will gain a new world but lose our souls until yet another opportunity comes, and the gates of infinity open wide to let that horseman in our midst.

Chapter Three

The Bearer of the Vision

O Lord, our Lord
How excellent is thy name in all the Earth,
Who hast set to thy glory above the heavens.
. . . When I consider thy heavens, the work of thy fingers,
The moon and the stars
Which thou hast ordained:
What is man, that thou art mindful of him?
And the son of man that thou visitest him?
For thou hast made him a little lower than the angels
And hast crowned him with glory and honour.
Thou madest him to have dominion over the works of thy hands
And thou hast put all things under his feet;
All sheep and oxen, yea, and the beasts of the field,
The fowl of the air and the fish of the sea
And whatsoever passeth through the paths of the seas.
O Lord, our Lord
How excellent is thy name in all the Earth.

'What is man,' the psalmist asks, 'that thou art mindful of him? For thou hast made him a little lower than the angels and hast crowned him with glory and honour.' Man has his beginnings in nameless, timeless, spaceless wonder. The only way that we can approach the mystery that is man is in the same way a child curled up before a fire perhaps on a rainy cold night listens to the words of the parent who is telling some marvellous tale, a tale of princes and princesses, of great soaring castles and magical lands. The child sits before the flames watching them sparkle and dance, and in the imagination of the child the images of the tale take form. Surely everyone at some time has experienced this sense of wonder, when we are transported beyond the confines of the concrete world, beyond the four walls that encompass us; and with a delightful feeling of warmth, a certain thrill of adventure, we allow our minds and hearts to travel.

It is in that spirit alone that we can approach the mystery of man and his origins. Just as the fairy land is real to the child though quite different from its ordinary surroundings, so the realms of man's true being, his homeland and his source, are real to us though quite different from the surroundings in which we presently perceive ourselves.

This reality plays an important part in our understanding of the New Age and of its externalization in our midst. For this age like any other is simply one stage upon a very long, in terms of time, processional of the unfoldment of the reality of man.

If one is to gaze upon a tree, where does one begin? Is it with the seed? Is it with the sapling? Is it with the full plant as it sends its branches out and grows? Where is the tree? The reality of the tree is present in all of these forms, and each of the forms represents simply another stage in the unfoldment of that reality. The same is true for man. The reality of man, approached only in wonder and a certain awe, is none the less unfolded through many stages and many forms of which we now approach yet another.

When this realm—physical, emotional, mental realm—was created, vast energies were called into being and harnessed. Ancient Greek philosophers set forth the theory of the atom, that single particle which is indivisible, the smallest bit of matter. This concept has been adopted in modern physical analyses of our universe; and yet within the past fifty years, certainly within the past twenty, the fields of nuclear research have demonstrated that we have yet to discover such a single ultimate particle. In fact what we are discovering are strange forms of energy that coincide with no known physical laws; qualities that are both waves and particles, both matter and energy at the same time; particles which can exist simultaneously in two different places; particles which can move from one point to another point without crossing the distance between. As nuclear science penetrates ever more deeply

34

into the mysteries of what used to be called the atom, we are confronted with an incredible mandala-like concentration or convergence of force, of life, of energy. We can analyze it and analyze it. The particles can be bombarded and split, and yet we have not touched upon that centre point that is actually holding all of this together.

What is this ultimate point, this presence, quality, energy which in this most minute world has gathered together these forces and holds them in such a relationship that all the macrocosmic worlds with which we are familiar can come into existence?

Here is a quality which is nameless and we cannot understand man unless we perceive that quality. A modern nuclear researcher is like a spinner of yarns of ancient times. He is a person who deals in fairy tales. Who ever heard of something like a particle that can exist in two places at the same time? Or a something or other that is both energy and matter simultaneously? It moves like a wave, like ripples upon a lake, and yet it moves like a ball that has been thrown through the air, and does so simultaneously. That is stuff of legend, of mystery, of wonder.

Consider the astronomer who, casting his nets of energy out into the universe, brings back to himself signatures of great radiating bodies, the quasars, which also seem to obey no known laws; radiating bodies that are putting forth energy at an incomprehensible level, and which seem to be neither star nor planet nor anything that man has yet come across. Astronomers too, deal in fairy tales, in the stuff of wonder and of magic.

Behind all this surely is a presence which laughs at man who considers that the universe is essentially known, that he is dwelling within a room the confines of which may be very large and he may not have explored all of its hidden nooks and crannies, yet for the most part he knows most of the interior decorating of that room.

The crisis of modern science lies in the simple fact that we are revealing a universe that does not conform to any known pattern of human thought, which may never conform to any known pattern of human thought; and which if it obeys laws at all, and apparently it does, obeys laws that are beyond the comprehensibility of finite mind. Science is like the parent, spinning a tale for the child sitting in front of the fire. Whether we know it or not our world is opening out into wonder, yet that wonder has always been with us. It exists within each of us and is the reality of man.

Drawing our attention then from the brief look at the great yarn spinner of modern scientific research, we come back to our original question, our original proposition: that to understand man we must give ourselves again the quality of awe and wonder, to open out like a child opens out in imagination. In imagination we go back to the time when this realm was created and these vast forces held in the most intricate of relationships within atomic matter were drawn together.

What is actually involved in such a task? What is involved in binding these forces in such a way that the world as we know it can come into existence? What must be at work within that invisible heart of the atom, working with laws which we cannot even begin to understand finitely because they do not operate within finite dimensions? That which can exist simultaneously in several places at once is not operating within a finite dimension. That which can move from one spot to another with no passage through space or time is not operating in a finite dimension. Yet that is the way the electron manifests itself.

What is at work there? What kind of intelligence? What kind of consciousness? What kind of understanding? In the immortal words of a great and mystic sage, 'the mind boggles.' What is at work there is the source from which we come, and the reality of it all is that, marvel upon marvel, it is *our* consciousness that is at work there. It is the seed potential of what is within *us* that is at work there.

When the creative forces were set into motion they were guided upon their way by a whole host of beings, on their smallest level fairy-like perhaps, but on their greatest level cosmic angelic beings for whom these laws both known and unknown are simply the rhythms of their own expression, the outworking of their breath. These beings, as we know them, are called angels, or devas. They are the builders. They are the intelligences that ensoul the energies which we find coming from the quasars and which we find enfolding the smallest particles yet known to man which some scientist, obviously with a sense of humour, called the quark. Great and small, all this energy is alive and is the manifestation of some form of living being, intelligent, conscious, aware, yet manifesting that awareness, that consciousness, that intelligence in many different ways.

So the image I wish to place in your minds is that of a host of lives who have responded to a creative impulse emerging from the creator, the source, and have acted upon that impulse. They have taken the basic note and have built infinite variations on its theme.

Pierre Teilhard de Chardin in his monumental works speaks of the processes of complexification, of building greater combinations from very small and simple particles. Most of the life that we know on this planet is basically built up from three simple atomic structures: hydrogen, carbon and oxygen. From these three simple atomic structures we gain the splendour and wonder of protoplasm and all that has been built from that simple yet amazingly complex substance.

So these beings move out and from a simple level begin to act and to act, to build and to build, to take into themselves and to give forth again, to create many combinations which in turn can be used for further combinations, and the world as we know it comes into being. The ancients spoke of this in very simple terms when they referred to the four great elements (fire, water, earth, and ether or air), the four elements from which all material expression is built up, and all spiritual expression too for that matter, with the spiritual counterparts of these elements; and this great host of beings who work within the elements, the builders, who are called elementals, although we have come to use the term in slightly different, more specified fashion.

In the midst of all this, in the presence of the host of angels so to speak, the word ensouled itself as a living idea. This can best be visualized if we go back to the analogy of the plant and see the rhythm of this growing thing as it emerges from a seed, and from that seed it creates all manner of forms, specialized cells, in order to do specialized tasks that permit a complex organism to exist: cells to absorb moisture and nourishment from the earth; cells to absorb sunlight and energy from the atmosphere; cells to absorb gas, cells to give off gas; cells to digest, cells to assimilate, cells to grow. And all of this fantastic complexity leads up essentially to one thing, a return to a very simple seed.

It is a statement that circulates among biologists and zoologists that all animal and plant life as we know it is simply a delivery system that allows the basic living matter of the germ plasm, the carrier of the genes, to propagate itself. In a sense this is so. If we carry this analogy back into our greater dimension, then this idea that was created to ensoul the word, the seed, comes forward to be the seed for new creation, for a new god, for a new birth in future time and future space. That seed is man: man as a living idea encompasses the heart and soul intent of the Creator who gave him form and carries that same ineffable, creative presence to a point where it can realize itself again in increasing splendour and power. Man as a living idea encompasses far more than we are at the moment, for we are a very simple stage along this processional.

The universe, or at least the solar system, as we know it, will one day have to break open metaphorically, perhaps physically too, like a great seed pod, before man reaches his fulfilment. Man, the living idea of man, known esoterically as the heavenly man, or the sum total of human lives, will move out from this solar system to create yet other worlds. Within this great unfoldment emerges man as we know him; two legs, two arms, a head and certain sensory patterns, certain systems of organs, physiology and neurology, emerging from the animal kingdom and being—what?

Many people believe that the theory of evolution is incorrect where man is concerned, for they cannot reconcile the quality and nature of man with the concept that all of this has evolved from the animal kingdom. They point to the Bible and to other scriptures, but particularly to the Bible, to indicate that man was especially created by God, and as the psalmist said, to have dominion over the Earth. This is true. Man as we know him, the idea of man, is an idea that has taken incarnation into a body a long time ago, but a body that was prepared for him.

When this occurred a link was established which had not existed previously, a link between three worlds: of matter, of form, the physical; the emotional and the mental; and the realm of spirit or soul, the comparitively or relatively formless world; and that which linked the two was the quality of mind. The occult definition of man, in whatever form he exists, is that he is the being who links the highest heaven and the lowest planes of matter through the instrumentality of mind, the energy of mind.

That definition itself only expresses one stage of the living idea of mankind. We are beings who at one point co-existed in full splendour with that original host from which this world was created. We are in essence, in origin, devic beings, angelic beings; and yet like any seed, the quality of a seed, the quality of the germ plasm of any organism is that it contains the whole, the wholeness of that organism. It does not contain just enough of the organism to make leaves, or just enough to make bark, or just enough to make flowers; it contains the entire genetic pattern of that species so that it can reproduce itself as a full-fledged member of that species.

Man must be considered in terms of consciousness, whereas many of the angelic builders are specialized beings manifesting a particular skill or work within the divine body. Man is a whole being, a composite being capable of manifesting the wholeness of the divine pattern.

Within you and within our collective wholeness is in microcosmic form wholeness of the Divine, of the Creator. Though at the moment we cannot function with the same power, the same love, the same attunement that many of the angelic forces are working with, we nevertheless contain within ourselves all that they are and more. According to Divina the devic consciousness sums up the New Age; it is what we are moving into. That is always what we are moving into, it is always what we are unfolding. It is our divine heritage, our angelic heritage that is being unfolded from us.

It is that consciousness, that life, which at the beginning of time as we know it had the capacity, the ability, the absolutely indescribable and awesome awareness to harness all of those forces of which we were speaking earlier, to make them work as they work, to make a universe such as we know possible. Unless we can capture the vision of this wonder within us, we will be hampered in our ability to unfold the next stage of human expression. It is important that we move not only with a vision of the next step but with a vision of what we are in our wholeness, in our source, in our centre.

What is it that is actually making that next step and why is that next step being made? It is written that a little child shall lead them. In the context in which this is stated it is used to refer to a quality of consciousness which can perceive the reality behind the apparent world; a quality of faith and trust and innocence and openness. But I want to interpret that in a different way. It is the seed that uplifts the plant, that carries the plant to its fulfilment. It is that which moves and grows and progresses that carries the whole to its fulfilment.

In Findhorn Community are many buildings and it is located upon the soil of Scotland; yet through these buildings and upon that soil are moving beings who are constantly changing, growing, living. They are not static like the buildings are. They are not apparently immobile like the soil is. Take all the people away from the buildings, off the soil, and where would the Community be? The glory, the potential, the meaning of Findhorn is in its people, not its land, not its buildings. It is in the life that moves through these things.

And yet the buildings and the land take on a special meaning, a special power, a certain significance, a certain holiness and wholesomeness because the people are there, and they are using it to manifest a living principle; and through the release of that principle into the environment the many lives, the intelligence, the awareness, the consciousness that is at present locked within concrete and stone and wood and plastic and fabric itself comes alive, itself unfolds, like in the old fairy tales where the magician makes the chair dance and the dishes wash themselves, and various inanimate objects become quite animate. The people are that magician. They call forth the life that is within apparently dead matter.

Man's position in the scheme of earthly evolution is that by being a bridge between matter and spirit, he provides the means for the life force to cross and to link the two and return to its source. Man upon the inbreath has moved into matter, upon the outbreath provides the means for matter to return to spirit. This is not just metaphorical knowledge. I am not spinning a tale. It is destined to come that as man himself transforms his being into its next stage, which could be called super-man, soul-man, man functioning not as a personality but as soul incarnate, so he possesses the capacity and will manifest that capacity to change the very force acting within the heart of atomic matter, to enable it to release greater and greater revelations of its inherent life and energy and light, until such time as all this world is spiritualized.

But for man to do this he must learn to be a good bridge. He must learn how to establish that contact, that centredness, that attunement with the whole, with his future, with his destiny. The seed must not lose contact with the vision of the reality that is behind it, otherwise it becomes just a seed. The potency of a seed lies not in its seediness but in its wholeness, the fact that the living image of the whole plant lives within it and acts within it.

Therefore man is asked to learn through physical form where he has the fullest contact with the results of creative expression, right here in the midst of a world, of an arena where creative law has its most tangible outworking, where cause and effect grinds on in its inexorable fashion, where everything is expanded in such a way that you can, standing outside of it, look at it and see the law in action and feel its impact upon your being. Here man must learn what it means to be a creator and the laws of his creativity which are the laws of his own being. The whole story of man's growth is the story of his learning of these laws, and the various epochs that have marked man's history are characterized by the way man has defined himself in relationship to these laws, in relationship to God. Has man seen himself as a child of Nature? Has man seen himself as a child of God? Has man seen himself a servant of God? Has man seen himself as the lord of the world? How man has defined himself has characterized the quality of his own creativity that he has allowed to be released into his world, and has therefore created the qualities of the ages through which he has moved.

Now, we say, a new age dawns; which means simply that man is gaining a new awareness of what he is and can take yet another step in the externalization of his seed potential. The New Age vision is at its heart a restatement of the nature and beingness of man. In some ways it is definitely a restatement, it has all been said before. In other ways it is new revelation, because now man has the capacity to act upon the definition of his spirituality in ways that were not his before because of the incoming of new energies and because of the cumulative effect of evolution which has sensitized his vehicles and now brings him to the brink of being able to function in the realm of thought with greater potency than he has ever been able to do before.

How will man define himself? Can he redefine himself? Can human nature be changed? Well, it has been changed throughout history. Human nature has not remained a steady, constant thing, and it is about to change again. The qualities that will determine its change, the energies that make it possible are summed up in the concepts of the great religious and philosophical teachings of the past—love, wisdom, compassion, light—and are indicated by the qualities of the new energies that are now entering, energies which demand of man that he become aware of his true nature, which is not an individualized nature but a group nature, which is only another way of saying that the consciousness of the soul is universal. It is intimately aware of itself as an individual but that awareness embraces other points of individuality. Therefore group expression is important, and the communication that enhances group expression is important.

Man is to learn that he is part of a whole and only through that learning will he gain the dominion that God has promised. Also through that learning he will be able to unleash certain of the building forces which are his natural birthright. Man now is doing with his mind what once a long time ago he did with his psychic powers, and which in the future that is just now beginning but which will unfold through thousands of years he will do with his soul. Man now manipulates matter. He taps the hidden forces of the atom. But he has always been able to do that through his soul and now will begin to learn again how to do it, how to be once more a builder.

The New Age, what we are talking about as the New Age, is largely a human experience. We are interpreting it in human terms: new society, new mankind, new consciousness, and certainly this has its validity. But the energies that are coming in are affecting all the kingdoms of life. They are having their impact in the plant kingdom, the animal kingdom, the mineral kingdom, the entire network is having its transformation.

But where is it all going to go? What is going to happen to it? How will it emerge into its fulfilment, its splendour? It emerges through that being who in his fullness is man, more than what we are at the moment and yet definitely what we are emerging into and will become, and indeed are now in our true centre, our essence. Man is the focal point now. The test of the age is focused upon humanity. Humanity is the world initiate about to undergo, in fact now undergoing, the crisis of initiation. All of this is placed upon man because he is the seed. Not that the other kingdoms do not contain the divine life in equal splendour, but because man is the only kingdom that has the capacity now to grow, to grow from within, to unfold from within like a seed, and not to grow because of the impact of exterior forces. The plant waits upon the rain and the sun and the soil for its growth, but man has a centre within himself that is the source of his nourishment and he need not wait upon any external force. By unleashing that inner centre he will nourish the wholeness of his world in ways undreamed of.

This is why man, who has taken angelic powers and encapsulated them within a certain intensity of development so that something other than an angelic consciousness can be made manifest, is given dominion over the Earth, dominion he has yet to demonstrate. This is why man is crowned with the glory of his seedship, his sonship, and it is why God, who has created all of this, is yet mindful of man.

The full mystery of what we are I cannot begin to express. I only hope that it is indicated to you; and yet that mystery is important. The wonder is important.

Beside the fire hearths of your own imagination may each explore the great cosmic yarn, the tale of marvel and of splendour, and know that that tale is of you, and that the New Age, whatever form it takes, is simply the further unravelling of that majestic drama.

CHAPTER
FOUR

The New Man

Man in legend has descended from great realms of light and power, but man in reality contains those realms within himself as his inheritance and as the very life force which he is in the process of unfolding. If we think of ourselves as unchanging beings, as the summit of evolution; if being involved in attempting to work with human nature, we think there can be no basic change in human nature, no fundamental alteration in the patterns that determine our behaviour, then we are in a real sense dead.

Yet that is the consciousness that many people operate on as a basic premise for their life: that growth takes place during a certain period roughly extending from birth to the age of twenty-five or so, and after that an individual has become fairly well set into his patterns and moulded by his society. He has become conditioned. You hear a lot about the impact of conditioning on a child during the first seven years. Like any good computer that has been programmed and set on its way and the programmer has wandered off and got lost someplace, there is nothing you can do other than unplug the machine—and death does that. The basic thought-form under which so many people work and order their lives is one of death, of non-growth, of seeking form, of seeking a static secure state.

As we have seen man cannot be considered under those terms. We can only approach that subject with a great sense of awe and wonder, with a sense

47

that the human being knows no end. Man is a seed. He is a being that is in the process of becoming. He is not a form, he is a process, he is a dynamic expression continually unfolding itself. He is the future incarnated, just as a seed is the tangible evidence of the future.

The tree is not the form, the tree is the seed, the sapling, the full grown plant and the seed that comes from it. Man is not the being that descended aeons ago into physical manifestation. He is not the animal form into which that spiritual life descended. He is not what we are now, nor is man what some people see as the super-human being as exemplified by the Hierarchy. Man is all of these things and none of these things. Man is beyond the forms that temporarily encase him, and we as representatives of man are beyond the forms that temporarily encase us. The true reality of our life is essentially one of limitlessness and of abundant potential, awaiting its tapping and its unfoldment. Chronological age, culture, nationality, past conditioning, really has nothing to do with it. There is no limitation upon what we can grow into except those that we create.

A great deal of research has been done in recent years to prove something which has been known in many ancient cultures and which has been part of our Christian heritage, summed up in the words, 'As a man thinketh, so he is.' But the words of prophets do not always carry the weight that one would like them to, and as a consequence we have had to prove this to ourselves mentally. For those who care to investigate the annals of psychological and sociological research, the proof is there and forms the basis for a new kind of psychology which is becoming very popular in America, called self-image psychology.

Some of its earliest exponents were people behind the psycho-cybernetics movement, but it goes much deeper than simply reprogramming oneself. It states that the way an individual defines himself determines how he will express his infinite beingness. At least that is my paraphrasing of what this states. To the extent that a person can respect himself, have a healthy esteem for himself, can in essence love himself, to that extent he can fulfil his divine potential. To the extent that he has a poor image of himself, he is burdened with unnecessary guilt—that is, guilt that has no rational cause in real life, but guilt that is culturally induced through mass acceptance of certain thought-forms such as original sin; people who feel that because of actions that they have taken, or that their parents have taken, or that their culture has taken, they are limited. Persons with that image do not grow, cannot unfold the divine that is within and cannot move into a greater consciousness, because they do not believe that they can. They are not accepting it for themselves. They have a basic image of unworth, lack of value.

The greatest indication to me that we are truly entering a new age lies in the fact that this basic thought pattern is being steadily challenged and destroyed, this thought pattern of limiting definitions of man. For example, it is a fairly widespread belief that man does not like to work, that man must be in some way threatened if he is going to grow or to move—the philosophy of the carrot and the stick, reward and punishment—that man's basic instinct is to seek security, is to seek safety, is to seek the known so that he is not threatened by the unknown, and that most people would much rather have someone else tell them what to do than decide for themselves.

Needless to say, having made those assumptions about human nature many people have gone to work to validate them and we have but to look upon society to see many examples that would indicate that that is a pretty fair description of the human race. Most Western business practices are based on that very assumption. There are time clocks to see that people come to work. There are punishments if they do not, there are rewards if they do. There are all kinds of motivations and methods that are generally designed to coerce consciousness.

However, increasing research indicates what has often been stated in the past and should have been self-evident, that as soon as certain rigid definitions as to what constitutes work and play are removed we find that man is not like that at all. Man has a need to work, a desire to grow, an actual inherent need for self-expression, for self-actualization; and if a person is in tune with a vision that person will give of themselves far more, work far harder, far longer, than a person who is simply punching a time clock. A person who has a time clock consciousness knows that he is doing in work what he does not really want to do. What he really wants to do is be out playing some place. As a consequence his consciousness is always anticipating the moment when the clock strikes five or four or whatever and he can go and do the things he really wants to do.

Our definition of man has created a weird economic state in which we work for a living in order that we can have the opportunity to play, rather than acknowledging a basic principle that work is love in action and nothing else, and for a person who is expressing that love, work and joy become one and the same. Work and play become identical. So you do not hasten away from your desk in order to go out and find pleasure, because you are finding it in the very achievement that you are creating.

The revolution in redefining what constitutes a human being is very significant, especially to people like ourselves who are entering the New Age from a somewhat more esoteric background; that is we believe ourselves to be in tune with presences and forces of a transcendent nature. We have before us the example of individuals called the masters, of the mahatmas or the elder brothers, who represent for us what human evolution can achieve in terms of unity with the whole. The various books of the occult and of the esoteric are filled with descriptions of what these masters are like.

I would like to quote from a book that is one of the standard textbooks for what is called Third Force Psychology that you may see the similarities. This is a book that is a text in most American universities, in psychology departments. It is called *Motivation and Personality*, second edition, by Abraham Maslow. Abraham Maslow was a pioneer in a field of research which was predicted a number of years ago (somewhere in the decade 1920–1930) by the Master Djwal Khul when he said that increasingly within the next fifty years science would begin to prove the existence of the soul and would so re-orient the human consciousness that man would realize that his true identity is the soul. It is not the personality, it is not the body, the mind, nor the emotions. Maslow was very definitely a pioneer in this work. He is the one who developed the concept of the self-actualized individual and laid the foundation for all later research in what is called humanistic psychology.

The basic premise on which he works is that in all forms of psychological research in the past we have studied sick people. As a consequence our image of humanity is based on the abnormal, which we have called the normal. Statistically we have called it the normal. By developing a psychology of non-integrated, non-whole, crippled personality, we have projected onto man a definition of himself which is equally non-whole, non-integrated and crippled. As a consequence how can man grow? He is continually trying to balance himself within forces that are essentially themselves out of balance, so you end up with well-balanced neurotics.

In his description of a self-actualized person's characteristics, Maslow finds a 'more efficient perception of reality and a more comfortable relations

50

with it.' This means very simply that this person sees it as it is. He is not projecting onto the world his own desires of what he would like the world to be; he is actually seeing it for what it is and he is seeing himself for what he is. And Maslow says: 'The consequence is that they live more in the real world of nature than in the man-made mass of concepts, abstractions, expectations, beliefs, and stereotypes that most people confuse with the world. They are therefore far more apt to perceive what is there rather than their own wishes, hopes, fears, anxieties, their own theories and beliefs, or those of their cultural group.'

These individuals, whom he calls the healthy types, 'are generally unthreatened and unfrightened by the unknown, being therein quite different from average men. They accept it, are comfortable with it, and, often are even *more* attracted by it than by the known. They not only tolerate the ambiguous and unstructured; they like it. Quite characteristic is Einstein's statement, "The most beautiful thing we can experience is the mysterious. It is the source of all art and science."' Echoes of Krishnamurti's teachings: freedom from the known, being able to accept and trust the creative processes of the divine life which so far transcend the mind that the mind cannot project forward and say, 'This is the way it is going to happen. This is what I will do. This is the way my future will manifest,' if that mind is going to be in tune with God, because the potentialities inherent in the divine are far more than the human mind can grasp. We have this experience in terms of having things develop for us, when we trust the life process, that generally are far more unfolding and beneficial than anything we would have predetermined for ourselves.

Another characteristic of self-actualized persons, persons who are living from the centre of the self, is that they accept themselves. It seems very basic. They accept themselves for what they are. They are not self-satisfied people, they are realistic people. They are not uptight about their physical being, their physical appetites, their emotional-mental natures. They see them for what they are. They accept them and they move to change them when they feel change may be required in order to promote growth.

What they do not do however is change themselves to suit society. They change themselves to suit the processes of inner growth and unfoldment. Such people have a great spontaneity and naturalness, Maslow has discovered, and he says, 'This does not necessarily mean consistently unconventional behavior. If we were to take an actual count of the number of times that the self-actualizing person behaved in an unconventional manner the tally would not be high. His unconventionality is not superficial but essential or internal. It is his impulses, thought, consciousness that are so unusually unconventional, spontaneous, and natural. Apparently recognizing that the world of people in which he lives could not understand or accept this, and since he has no wish to hurt them or to fight with them over every triviality, he will go through the ceremonies and rituals of convention with a good-humored shrug and with the best possible grace. Thus I have seen a man accept an honor he laughed at and even despised in private, rather than make an issue of it and hurt the people who thought they were pleasing him.

'That this conventionality is a cloak that rests very lightly upon his shoulders and is easily cast aside can be seen from the fact that the self-actualizing person infrequently allows convention to hamper him or inhibit him from doing anything that he considers very important or basic. It is at such moments that his essential lack of conventionality appears, and not as with the average Bohemian or authority-rebel, who makes great issues of trivial things and who will fight against some unimportant regulations as if it were a world issue.'

Findings have 'led ultimately to the discovery of a most profound difference between self-actualizing people and others; namely, that the motivational life of self-actualizing people is not only quantitatively different but also qualitatively different from that of ordinary people. It seems probable that we must construct a profoundly different psychology of motivation for self-actualizing people, e.g., metamotivation or growth motivation, rather than deficiency motivation. ... Our subjects no longer strive in the ordinary sense, but rather develop. They attempt to grow to perfection and to develop more and more fully in their own style. The motivation of ordinary men is a striving for the basic need gratifications that they lack. But self-actualizing people in fact lack none of these gratifications. ... They work, they try, and they are ambitious, even though in an unusual sense. For them motivation is just character growth, character expression, maturation, and development.'

Such people are 'strongly focused on problems outside themselves. ... They are problem centered rather than ego centered. They generally are not problems for themselves and are not generally much concerned about themselves; e.g., as contrasted with the ordinary introspectiveness that one finds in insecure people. These individuals customarily have some mission in life, some task to fulfil, some problem outside themselves which enlists much of their energies.

'This is not necessarily a task that they would prefer or choose for themselves; it may be a task that they feel is their responsibility, duty, or obligation.' They have a keen and strong sense of responsibility to the good of the whole.

'With a few exceptions we can say that our objects are ordinarily concerned with basic issues and eternal questions of the type that we have learned to call philosophical or ethical. Such people live customarily in the widest possible frame of reference. They seem never to get so close to the trees that they fail to see the forest. They work within a framework of values that are broad and not petty, universal and not local, and in terms of a century rather than the moment. In a word, these people are all in one sense or another philosophers, however homely.' The tasks that they set themselves 'are nonpersonal or unselfish, concerned rather with the good of mankind in general, or of a nation in general, of a few individuals in the subject's family.'

Maslow says that 'in social relations with most people, detachment creates certain troubles and problems. It is easily interpreted by "normal" people as coldness, snobbishness, lack of affection, unfriendliness, or even hostility. By contrast, the ordinary friendship relationship is more clinging, more demanding, more desirous of reassurance, compliment, support, warmth, and exclusiveness. It is true that self-actualizing people do not need others in the ordinary sense. But since this being needed or being missed is the usual earnest of friendship, it is evident that detachment will not easily be accepted by average people.' They generally are independent of their given culture. which simply means that they have the capacity to act as their own agent if the need arises. They are not conditioned by the culture in which they have grown up, although they may accept it and work within it, yet should the need arise they can just as easily work beyond it.

'Deficiency-motivated people *must* have other people available, since most of their main need gratification (love, safety, respect, prestige, belongingness) can come only from other human beings. But growth-motivated people may actually be *hampered* by others. The determinants of satisfaction and of the good life are for them now inner-individual and *not* social. They have become strong enough to be independent of the good opinion of other people, or even of their affection. The honors, the status, the rewards, the popularity, the prestige, and the love they can bestow must have become less important than self-development and inner growth. . . .'

These people 'have the wonderful capacity to appreciate again and again, freshly and naively, the basic goods of life, with awe, pleasure, wonder, and even ecstasy, however stale these experiences may have become to others. . . . Thus for such a person, any sunset may be as beautiful as the first one, any flower may be of breath-taking loveliness, even after he has seen a million flowers. . . . He remains as convinced of his luck in marriage thirty years after his marriage and is as surprised by his wife's beauty when she is sixty as he was forty years before. For such people, even the casual workaday, moment-to-moment business of living can be thrilling, exciting and ecstatic.' They are given to peak experiences which in the past have been called mystic experiences and they are given to them because they do not deny them, they accept them, they are not frightened by them, they are not terrified by a sudden expansion of their being into an oceanic blending with all of life.

'. . . They have for human beings in general a deep feeling of identification, sympathy, and affection in spite of the occasional anger, impatience, or disgust described below. Because of this they have a genuine desire to help the human race. It is as if they were all members of a single family. One's feelings toward his brothers would be on the whole affectionate, even if these brothers were foolish, weak, or even if they were sometimes nasty. They would still be more easily forgiven than strangers. . . . When it comes down to it, in certain basic ways . . . (the self-actualizing person) is like an alien in a strange land. . . . He is often saddened, exasperated, and even enraged by the shortcomings of the average person, and while they are to him ordinarily no more than a nuisance, they sometimes become bitter tragedy. However far apart he is from them at times, he nevertheless feels a basic underlying kinship with these creatures whom he must regard with, if not condescension, at least the knowledge that he can do many things better than they can, that he can see things that they cannot see, that the truth that is so clear to him is for most people veiled and hidden. This is what Adler called the older-brotherly attitude.' They generally have 'deeper and more profound interpersonal relationships than any other adults (although not necessarily deeper than those of children).'

He says that a child is a very good example of such a person—not all children, but most children. 'They are capable of more fusion, greater love, more perfect identification, more obliteration of the ego boundaries than other people would consider possible. There are, however, certain special characteristics of these relationships. . . . It is my observation that the other members of these relationships are likely to be . . . closer to self-actualization than the average. . . .' These people exercise a high selectiveness and generally have very, very few friends. The exclusiveness of their devotion to a very few people can and does exist side by side with a wide-spreading love, benevolence, affection and friendliness for all of mankind. 'These people *tend* to be kind or at least patient to almost everyone. . . . In a very real . . . sense they love or rather have compassion for all mankind. This love does not imply lack of discrimination. The fact is that they can and do speak realistically and harshly of those who deserve it. . . .' But the face-to-face relationships that they have with those people who would deserve such things 'do not always show signs of realistically low evaluations.'

One such subject explained this as follows: '"Most people, after all, do not amount to much but they *could* have. They make all sorts of foolish mistakes and wind up being miserable and not knowing how they got that way when their intentions were good. Those who are not nice are usually paying for it in deep unhappiness. They should be pitied rather than attacked."

'Perhaps the briefest possible description is to say that their hostile reactions to others are (1) deserved, (2) for the good of the person attacked or for someone else's good.' That is to say their hostility is not based against a character but is to enhance or to clarify a situation.

They are democratic in that they make no distinctions as to class or nationality or creed or economic level. 'I have found none of my subjects to be chronically unsure about the difference between right and wrong in his actual living. Whether or not they could verbalize the matter, they rarely showed in their day-to-day living the chaos, the confusion, the inconsistency, or the conflict that are so common in the average person's ethical dealings. This may be phrased also in the following terms: these individuals are strongly ethical, they have definite moral standards, they do right and do not do wrong. Needless to say, their notions of right and wrong and of good and evil are often not the conventional ones.' Their humour—and most all have a sense of humour—is not hostile, but more philosophical in nature. They are all creative, though the creativity is not necessarily that of genius. It is that of being able to get the fullness out of life. They can have as many imperfections as any other person. The thing is they are not hung-up by them, and move to change them when such imperfections are an obstacle to the externalization of their greatest potential. Such people 'are occasionally capable of an extraordinary and unexpected ruthlessness. . . . This makes it possible for them to display a surgical coldness when this is called for, beyond the power of the average man. The man who found that a long-trusted acquaintance was dishonest cut himself off from this friendship sharply and abruptly and without any observable pangs whatsoever.' Some of these people recover so quickly from the death of people close to them as to appear heartless to others. That action, incidentally, is listed under the topic heading, 'The Imperfections of Self-Actualizing People.'

'At this point we may finally allow ourselves to generalize and underscore a very important theoretical conclusion. . . . It was concluded that what had been considered in the past to be polarities or opposites or dichotomies . . . were resolved, the polarities disappeared, and many oppositions thought to be intrinsic merged and coalesced with each other to form unities.' These people are essentially holistic. They create unity within themselves. For example the age-old opposition between heart and head, reason and instinct, mentality and emotion, would seem to disappear in healthy people and these two aspects become synergic—which simply means they contribute to each other—rather than antagonistic. 'The dichotomy between selfishness and unselfishness disappears altogether . . . because in principle every act is *both* selfish and unselfish. Our subjects are simultaneously very spiritual . . . and sensual. . . . Duty cannot be contrasted with pleasure nor work with play when duty *is* pleasure, when work *is* play, and the person doing his duty and being virtuous is simultaneously seeking his pleasure and being happy.' The higher and lower aspects of these people are not in opposition with themselves—they are in agreement 'and a thousand serious philosophical dilemmas are discovered to have . . . no horns at all. If the war between the sexes (for example) turns out to be no war at all in matured people, but only a sign of crippling and stunting of growth, who then would wish to choose sides?'

Maslow concludes that 'healthy people are so different from average ones, not only in degree but in kind as well, that they generate two very different kinds of psychology. It becomes more and more clear that the study of crippled, stunted, immature, and unhealthy specimens can yield only a cripple psychology and a cripple philosophy. The study of self-actualizing people must be the basis for a more universal science of psychology.'

Most of what has been described by Maslow is the same description that is given to a master, with certain variations. It is also the description of what a human being truly is. This is incredibly important because it represents a break from the definitions of the past, at least the Western definitions of the past, and in many cases some of the Eastern ones too; an admission that what is walking around inside this fleshy skin on two legs is a good deal more than most people have ever given it credit for being. That is a fundamental premise for entering into the New Age.

How does one become a self-actualized person? Some of the techniques that Maslow describes might as well have been listed from books on meditation or yoga or the spiritual life. One means is through living each moment with as much awareness as possible. One means is by pouring love through that awareness into everything you do. Is that sounding familiar? One way that he gave to a group of psychologists, psychologist trainees, is to have the courage to face the unknown, the courage to be one's self, courage to grow, to go within and determine what you really want to do and not what other people tell you you should do and then do it, work at it, work hard at it, discipline yourself and get into the rhythm that comes from such accomplishments and unfoldment.

But most importantly, the distinction between this kind of person and the other kind of person is brought out in the words that were used: one who is deficiency-motivated and one who is growth-motivated. Here we say: one who acts out of lack and one who acts out of a sense of abundance. It is the basic difference between the old laws of manifestation and the new laws of manifestation. Do we perceive lack which we attempt to fill? Or do we perceive abundance which we seek to make manifest and to generate?

The deficiency-motivated person is just that. He is aware that he is deficient and sees his environment simply as a storehouse where by hook or by crook he can make up his deficiency. A growth-motivated person sees that all is within him; the environment is the arena, the helpmate, the midwife, the womb, the Beloved, that can help all of that to unfold in progressive measure.

Just a little change like that, a little realization, a little redefinition of what man is: that man is not a being who hates to work, who is filled with these lacks, who is condemned to a certain sinful position relative to the whole; but man is the seed presence of the infinite, that what is within us, what lives within us, is something that can only be approached in great love and awe and wonder, no matter what we do with it, no matter what mistakes we have made. If we have made them we can learn from them and use them as stepping stones to further realization.

Maslow is very careful to point out that the self-actualizing person can at times be every bit as pigheaded and stupid as the ordinary Joe and make errors of judgement. The thing is that he learns from that, grows from it and is not burdened by unnecessary guilt. They do have guilts but their guilts come from failures to enable themselves to grow. For example, if you know you have a talent and you know you could be expressing it, but you are too lazy to do it, that gives you guilt. Within the context of the New Age vision this image of mankind is what needs to be communicated, and it is communicated by example as well as through words—in fact, primarily through example.

The whole movement of humanistic psychology grew from the fact that Maslow as a student found himself in the presence of some very remarkable people and he suddenly realized that for all their uniqueness there were certain definite things they had in common and he wondered if there were other such super-healthy people about. This started him on this research which engaged him throughout most of his life. He is describing not an aim, not a goal, like some people read esoteric books that describe the masters and they feel, 'Well, that's a nice goal, it's nice to think that maybe those beings exist.' He is describing real people, everyday people he has met, people he has worked with, people from housewives with no chance to go beyond not even a high school education to people with a long string of degrees after their names who are leaders in various fields. He is describing a reality, just as Findhorn is manifesting a reality. The reality of the action and presence of God in human life.

The humanistic psychology movement in its highest form—it has its lunatic fringe but in the form that is being expressed by Maslow—is incredibly close, in fact it is nothing more than a restatement of the same things that the New Age movement is seeking to convey to people. But how much of the New Age movement is based on deficiency-motivation? How much of the

New Age is being viewed as simply that which we lack, and that which by hook or crook we better get—higher consciousness, the presence of more evolved beings, light, love, and all the rest of it.

What Maslow is saying is that those who are true prototypes of the new humanity are those who do not see this lack in themselves, but know that in our terminology they *are* the New Age, and they had better get up and start actualizing it, expressing it, bringing it out, growing, externalizing it, being it.

The great scientific revolutions of the past few decades are motivating man into a new society, but no revolution or evolution is quite as significant as this one which is taking place—the redefinition of the true nature of man.

For centuries we have worked and struggled under a short-sighted view of what we are. We have set our sights at too low a level of defining the nature of man. Because man is as he thinks, we have fulfilled all too ably that inadequate definition. We have made it come to pass. Now with many opportunities about us we can make a new definition come to pass in our own lives and in the lives of the communities that we create and in our world, a new humanity from which can spring a new heaven and a new Earth.

From Krishna to Christ

The New Age consciousness is really quite old and the demonstration of human capability and super-human capability has always been with us. The teachings of the past form the foundation from which the new is emerging.

In this chapter I want to trace some of these traditions, particularly those from the life and teachings of Buddha. There is a theme to this other than an historical one; in fact, the historical part will be the least of all because that is not really my intent. The theme is that throughout history the doctrine of sacrifice and renunciation has been held before humankind as one of the paths to the divine. It is indeed a path of great power, but it is also a path that is not very well understood. Jesus demonstrated five great initiatory steps, one in particular being that of the crucifixion. But the crucifixion has also been demonstrated by other religious leaders. The whole life of Buddha was a crucifixion or, as it is known in Eastern terms, the great renunciation.

Man has sensed that there is a power contained in the act of self-sacrifice that is not found in any other form of consciousness or action. Why is this so? In Western culture it has become a point of, to my mind, morbid focus, because we have concentrated on suffering and have in a very subtle way robbed the sacrificial act of its redeeming power. But the answer to this fascination which man has for sacrifice is not because there is a morbid streak in him, but because the secret of man's own being, the nature of man's own identity, is best understood within terms of the great renunciation.

I am greatly indebted to Sir Edwin Arnold in his two classical works, *Song Celestial* which is a translation of the Bhagavad-Gita, and *Light of Asia* which is a poetic rendition of the life of Siddartha, the Buddha. I want to quote from the Bhagavad-Gita simply to illustrate the timelessness of what we are calling the New Age vision and also to introduce certain other doctrines which will be important to our understanding.

In chapter four of the Bhagavad-Gita, Krishna, the divine incarnation who is posing as the charioteer of Arjuna, who is a prince, is answering questions for the prince. They are actually on a battlefield, the prince facing battle with his various relatives and clansmen who have usurped his throne, and Krishna states:

> Manifold the renewals of my birth
> Have been, Arjuna! and of thy births, too!
> But mine I know, and thine thou knowest not,
> O Slayer of thy Foes! Albeit I be
> Unborn, undying, indestructible,
> The Lord of all things living; not the less—
> By Maya, by my magic which I stamp
> On floating Nature-forms, the primal vast—
> I come, and go, and come. When Righteousness
> Declines, O Bharata! when Wickedness
> Is strong, I rise, from age to age, and take
> Visible shape, and move a man with men,
> Succouring the good, thrusting the evil back,
> And setting Virtue on her seat again.

Here two doctrines are enunciated: 'Albeit I be unborn, undying, indestructible, the Lord of all things living ... (yet) by my magic which I stamp on floating Nature-forms ... I come, and go, and come.' The all, the one, the infinite, dispersing itself into the many, into the manifold ... I create the universe and infuse it with myself, but still I remain. ... All things that we see, all things that are, are the manifestation of the one, which yet moves from its point of oneness and enters into diversity, manifold incarnations. This represents the first, the source, sacrifice.

Then we have the doctrine of the avatars: 'When Righteousness declines ... when Wickedness is strong, I rise, from age to age, and take visible shape, and move a man with men, succouring the good, thrusting the evil back, and setting Virtue on her seat again.' It is this doctrine which is used particularly in the esoteric schools, to support the proclamation that we are now again in a time of new revelation and new divine incarnation.

Later on in the Bhagavad-Gita, Krishna says, discussing one of the forms of yoga, the yoga of love and faith:

> Who hateth nought
> Of all which lives, living himself benign,
> Compassionate, from arrogance exempt,
> Exempt from love of self, unchangeable
> By good or ill; patient, contented, firm
> In faith, mastering himself, true to his word,
> Seeking Me, heart and soul; vowed unto Me,—
> That man I love! Who troubleth not his kind,
> And is not troubled by them; clear of wrath,
> Living too high for gladness, grief, or fear,
> That man I love! Who, dwelling quiet-eyed,
> Stainless, serene, well-balanced, unperplexed,
> Working with Me, yet from all works detached,
> That man I love! Who, fixed in faith on Me,
> Dotes upon none, scorns none; rejoices not,
> And grieves not, letting good or evil hap
> Light when it will, and when it will depart,
> That man I love! Who, unto friend and foe
> Keeping an equal heart, with equal mind
> Bears shame and glory; with an equal peace
> Takes heat and cold, pleasure and pain; abides
> Quit of desires, hears praise or calumny
> In passionless restraint, unmoved by each;
> Linked by no ties to earth, steadfast in Me,
> That man I love! But most of all I love
> Those happy ones to whom 'tis life to live
> In single fervid faith and love unseeing,
> Drinking and blessed Amrit of my Being!

This is, of course, a very ancient writing. The Vedas are source material of the religions that came later, including Christianity and Buddhism, and represent one of the first clear enunciations of the principles of man's at-one-ment with God, his potential experience and realization of that at-one-ment, and the qualities of being centred and free which lead to that realization.

But Hinduism degenerated as a religious form and became an expression of superstition, of caste, of power, and became a weight upon the people who lived within its realms. One of the teachings of Hinduism, which later became solidified, crystallized, was that of the caste. It developed into an hereditary pattern in which only the highest caste, the Brahmans, were able to experience the realms of spirit. Through the laws of reincarnation, if you were a good man in a life, eventually you would be privileged to be born as a Brahman. If you were not particularly good, you went down the scale in the other direction and ended up an untouchable—human beings who were quite literally outcasts from human society, being considered cursed. No member of the Indian social structure would socialize with these individuals. Of course if you went lower than that, you ended up something else—a snake, a bee, an ant—for the Hindus believed in transmigration of souls which is, however, not an occult or esoteric doctrine.

Into this came a man who was born into the princely warrior caste. He lived in a social condition very much equivalent to that enjoyed by a feudal Scottish lord. For at that time India was not united but was divided up into various feudal territories governed by various clans. Siddartha Gautama was his name. His life, as he became known as the awakened one, the illumined one, the Buddha, is known in the East as the great renunciation, for his entire life was a demonstration of giving up; at the same time it was a true demonstration that renunciation is really the path to the whole, to the all.

There are many legends concerning the Buddha, the usual birth legends concerning the phenomena that attended his birth, and the dreams and portents that went with it. But when he was born, the king, his father, sent for various wise men to read the signs and the portents. It was prophesied that this son had an ambiguous destiny. He could either become the greatest king that India would ever know, conquering all other feudal lords and placing India under the reign of one government, or he would become a penniless beggar who would redeem the world. One of the wise men who the king summoned, seeing the babe in the arms of its mother, fell upon his face and exclaimed:

> 'I worship! Thou are He!
> I see the rosy light, the foot-sole marks,
> The soft curled tendril of the Swastika,
> The sacred primal signs thirty and two,
> The eighty lesser tokens. Thou art Buddh,
> And thou wilt preach the Law and save all flesh
> Who learn the Law, though I shall never hear,

Dying too soon, who lately longed to die;
Howbeit I have seen Thee. Know, O King!
This is that Blossom on our human tree
Which opens once in many myriad years—
But opened, fills the world with Wisdom's scent
And Love's dropped honey.'

The king did not particularly like these prophecies. He was happy enough that they were prophesying a glorious future for his son, but he did not want his son to become a penniless beggar. So he set about to insure that the prince would indeed grow to inherit the throne and become the great king of India. You may be familiar with the story of how he was given the fairest maiden in all the land to be his wife and they lived in a pleasure palace where only perfect specimens of humanity could enter, and there could be no sign of age, of death, of disease, of discord, of ugliness of any kind. All day long there would be nothing but beautiful dancing and beautiful music and the best of foods and drinks, everything that would appeal to the senses of the prince so that he would remain contented and eventually become a king.

However, the best laid plans of mice and kings oft go astray. The king, poor man, had some rather powerful opponents working against his wishes, such as the wind devas. Short of closing the windows and suffocating the prince, he did not have much way of keeping the wind devas out. Then one day, one of the maidens who played the lutes and the sitars, laid her sitar upon the windowsill; a wind deva came by and played a tune upon it. To human ears all that one could hear would be the wind plucking the strings and causing them to vibrate, but Siddartha could hear a voice. Prince Siddartha heard the devas play, and to his ears they sang such words as these:

We are the voices of the wandering wind,
Which moan for rest and rest can never find;
Lo! as the wind is, so is mortal life,
A moan, a sigh, a sob, a storm, a strife.

Wherefore and whence we are ye cannot know,
Nor where life springs, nor whither life doth go;
We are as ye are, ghosts from the inane,
What pleasure have we of our changeful pain?

What pleasure hast thou of thy changeless bliss?
Nay, if love lasted, there were joy in this;
But life's way is the wind's way, all these things
Are but brief voices breathed on shifting strings.

O Maya's son! because we roam the earth
Moan we upon these strings; we make no mirth,
So many woes we see in many lands,
So many streaming eyes and wringing hands.

Yet mock we while we wail, for could they know,
This life they cling to is but empty show;
'Twere all as well to bid a cloud to stand,
Or hold a running river with the hand.

But thou that art to save, thine hour is nigh!
The sad world waiteth in its misery,
The blind world stumbleth on its round of pain;
Rise, Maya's child! wake! slumber not again!

We are the voices of the wandering wind:
Wander thou, too, O Prince, thy rest to find;
Leave love for love of lovers, for woe's sake
Quit state for sorrow, and deliverance make.

So sigh we, passing o'er the silver strings,
To thee who know'st not yet of earthly things;
So say we; mocking, as we pass away,
These lovely shadows wherewith thou dost play.

This gave Siddartha pause to think, and feeling that if he was going to be king he really ought to know something about the realm which he would rule over, he persuaded his father to let him out of the pleasure palace. This pleasure palace was locked in with three gates and there were guards over the gates. Furthermore, the gates were very large brass doors of which they never oiled the hinges, so that when they were opened they squeaked and groaned and shrieked so the king would always know if anyone entered or left the palace.

He realized that he could not say no to his son, so he sent word out that messengers were to go ahead and clear the city of all signs of ugliness and disease, of old age, of death, and only happy, beautiful people were to be present; banners were to be hung, the streets were to be cleaned. So the prince went forth.

There is a story of the four sights that he saw on his journey and on subsequent ones, either by them being overlooked or because gods incarnated in these forms. The prince saw an aged man, a diseased man and a dead man. Then he saw a monk in his orange robe with his begging bowl. These sights made the prince realize that all the things of the senses were passing, that though he had every pleasure that mortal man could conceive of, they could not keep him from growing old, from becoming sick or from dying. And by seeing the monk he realized that there was a way out of this. He could withdraw from the world and become a monk.

Siddartha turned
Eyes gleaming with divine tears to the sky,
Eyes lit with heavenly pity to the earth;
From sky to earth he looked, from earth to sky,
As if his spirit sought in lonely flight
Some far-off vision, linking this and that,
Lost—past—but searchable, but seen, but known.
Then cried he, while his lifted countenance
Glowed with the burning passion of a love
Unspeakable, the ardour of a hope
Boundless, insatiate: 'Oh! suffering world;
Oh! known and unknown of my common flesh,
Caught in this common net of death and woe,
And life which binds to both! I see, I feel
The vastness of the agony of earth,
The vainness of its joys, the mockery
Of all its best, the anguish of its worst;
Since pleasures end in pain, and youth in age,
And love in loss, and life in hateful death,
And death in unknown lives, which will but yoke
Men to their wheel again to whirl the round
Of false delights and woes that are not false.
Me too this lure hath cheated, so it seemed
Lovely to live, and life a sunlit stream
For ever flowing in a changeless peace;
Whereas the foolish ripple of the flood
Dances so lightly down by bloom and lawn
Only to pour its crystal quicklier
Into the foul salt sea. The veil is rent
Which blinded me! I am as all these men
Who cry upon their gods and are not heard,
Or are not heeded—yet there must be aid!
For them and me and all there must be help!
Perchance the gods have need of help themselves,
Being so feeble that when sad lips cry
They cannot save! I would not let one cry
Whom I could save! How can it be that Brahm
Would make a world and keep it miserable,

Since, if, all-powerful, he leaves it so,
He is not good, and if not powerful,
He is not God?'
Late one night he awakes and knows the time has come when he must
be about his mission. The following is a passage, a monologue that he speaks
to himself as he stands beside his window late at night:
'I will depart,' he spake; 'the hour is come!
Thy tender lips, dear Sleeper, summon me
To that which saves the earth but sunders us;
And in the silence of yon sky I read
My fated message flashing. Unto this
Came I, and unto this all nights and days
Have led me; for I will not have that crown
Which may be mine: I lay aside those realms
Which wait the gleaming of my naked sword:
My chariot shall not roll with bloody wheels
From victory to victory, till earth
Wears the red record of my name. I choose
To tread its paths with patient, stainless feet,
Making its dust my bed, its loneliest wastes
My dwelling, and its meanest things my mates;
Clad in no prouder garb than outcasts wear,
Fed with no meats save what the charitable
Give of their will, sheltered by no more pomp
Than the dim cave lends or the jungle-bush.
This will I do because the woeful cry
Of life and all flesh living cometh up
Into my ears, and all my soul is full
Of pity for the sickness of this world;
Which I will heal, if healing may be found
By uttermost renouncing and strong strife.
For which of all the great and lesser gods
Have power or pity? Who hath seen them—who?
What have they wrought to help their worshippers?
. . . None—not the worthiest—from the griefs that teach
Those litanies of flattery and fear
Ascending day by day, like wasted smoke?
Hath any of my brothers 'scaped thereby
The aches of life, the stings of love and loss,
The fiery fever and the ague-shake,
The slow, dull, sinking into withered age,
The horrible dark death—and what beyond

Waits—till the whirling wheel comes up again,
And new lives bring new sorrows to be borne,
. . . So are we kin
To all that is; and thus, if one might save
Man from his curse, the whole wide world should share
The lightened horror of this ignorance
Whose shadow is still fear, and cruelty
Its bitter pastime. Yea, if one might save!
And means must be! There must be refuge!
. . . What good gift have my brothers, but it came
From search and strife and loving sacrifice?
If one, then being great and fortunate,
Rich, dowered with health and ease, from birth designed
To rule—if he would rule—a King of kings;
If one, not tired with life's long day but glad
I' the freshness of its morning, one not cloyed
With love's delicious feasts, but hungry still;
If one not worn and wrinkled, sadly sage,
But joyous in the glory and the grace
That mix with evils here, and free to choose
Earth's Loveliest at his will: one even as I,
Who ache not, lack not, grieve not, save with griefs
Which are not mine, except as I am man;—
If such a one, having so much to give,
Gave all, laying it down for love of men,
And thenceforth spent himself to search for truth,
Wringing the secret of deliverance forth,
Whether it lurks in hells or hide in heavens,
Or hover, unrevealed, nigh unto all:
Surely at last, far off, sometime, somewhere,
The veil would lift for his deep-searching eyes,
The road would open for his painful feet,
That should be won for which he lost the world,
And Death might find him conqueror of death.
This will I do, who have a realm to lose,
Because I love my realm, because my heart
Beats with each throb of all the hearts that ache,
Known and unknown, these that are mine and those
Which shall be mine, a thousand million more
Saved by this sacrifice I offer now.
Oh, summoning stars! I come! Oh, mournful earth:
For thee and thine I lay aside my youth,

My throne, my joys, my golden days, my nights,
My happy palace—and thine arms, sweet Queen!
Harder to put aside than all the rest!
Yet thee, too, I shall save, saving this earth;
And that which stirs within thy tender womb,
My child, the hidden blossom of our loves,
Whom if I wait to bless my mind will fail.
Wife! child! father! and people! ye must share
A little while the anguish of this hour
That light may break and all flesh learn the Law.
Now am I fixed, and now I will depart,
Never to come again, till what I seek
Be found.'

It was this giving up of so much that causes his life to be called the great renunciation. He did go forth and he spent six years in search. He spent the first part of that time with Hindu sages learning the spiritual law. He spent the middle period of that time with a band of wandering ascetics, men who practiced the most strenuous forms of self-mutilation and denial to try and purge the body of its grip upon the spirit—everything short of death. And he outdid them all. At one point he fell into a stupor, and it was only because someone chanced by with some food that he was saved from dying. He realized that such strict asceticism was not the way, because it had not gained him enlightenment. It had just made him thin and starving and filled with aches and pains. So he gave it up and earned the curses of those who were following him. Then he went into a period of silent meditation, following practices similar to that of Raja Yoga, until eventually, knowing that the time was nigh he sat down beneath a fig tree which was called the Bodhi-tree—this is not its generic name, but it comes from the same root that Buddha comes from, meaning the tree of enlightenment, because under that tree he became the Buddha and he vowed never to get up again until he was the Buddha, the awakened one.

In a scene very reminiscent of Jesus' temptation in the wilderness, the devil came with his train of sins and tempted him; but he could not sway Siddartha from his path. He became the Buddha, pierced through to the heart of the universe and understood all things:

'Many a House of life
Hath held me—seeking ever him who wrought
These prisons of the senses, sorrow-fraught;

Sore was my ceaseless strife!
But now,
Thou Builder of this Tabernacle—Thou!
I know Thee! Never shalt Thou build again
These walls of pain,
Nor raise the roof-tree of deceits, nor lay
Fresh rafters on the clay;
Broken Thy house is, and the ridge-pole split!
Delusion fashioned it!
Safe pass I thence—deliverance to obtain.'

Then the devil gave him a unique temptation. He said, 'All right, I have failed. You are the Buddha. I could not tempt you and so I worship you. But really, you have gained such knowledge and such illumination and you have now become so far beyond the average mass of humanity, that no one will understand what you are talking about. If you go forth to preach your message, who will know what you are saying? So why do you not just go all the way and slip into Nirvana, into the all, and forget about Earth. Let me have the Earth and humanity and you go on and do your thing, being one with God.' (I paraphrased the devil's speech a little bit there.) Buddha thought about this and he almost accepted but finally he said, 'Well, no, there will be a few at least who will understand what I have to say.' This is the second reason why his life was called the great renunciation, because he stood at the brink of perfect and unending bliss and renounced it in order to remain in the world of humanity, that others might find the path.

His teaching is familiar to most people now: the Four Noble Truths of the existence of suffering, the cause of suffering and what can be done to release it. What can be done to release it is called the Eightfold Path, the practice of various principles, such as right thought, right speech, right behaviour, right aspiration, and so on. He preached for forty-five years after his illumination and became in his lifetime certainly one of the most popular of the world redeemers that has ever lived. He certainly reformed the Hindu religion.

The concept of suffering or of sacrifice and renunciation has been a powerful one on man's imagination. One reason for this may lie in an understanding of man himself. A great deal has been written concerning the allegorical implications of the life of Jesus: how the birth, the baptism, the transfiguration and the crucifixion all may be interpreted in terms of soul experiences that each individual must go through. But I have never actually seen anything written concerning the allegorical implications of Buddha's life. Yet Buddha too set down a pattern life, but not for an individual. He set forward a pattern insight into the human condition.

Let us look at the salient elements of Buddha's life. He was born a prince and he was surrounded by all things that could make him happy. He lived in what was called the palace of paradise, and he was cut off from ordinary humanity, from the rest of the world by three golden gates, or at least three large gates. He was not allowed to know anything of the conditions of the world. But the world, through humanity and through Nature, through the devas of the wind and of the earth and of the sea and of the growing things, cried out to him and spoke of their sorrow and of their pain and of the state of tension that they were in because of their physical condition. So he renounced paradise, moved through the three gates and became one with this world, understood it and gained illumination. Buddha is the avatar of wisdom who paves the way, esoterically, for the avatar of love-wisdom who is the Christ.

This, allegorically speaking, is a very accurate presentation of humanity if we consider humanity as a single being, which esoterically it is—the great initiate. There are undoubtedly a number of reasons why mankind took up physical form. Mostly we are told it was in the course of evolution to learn about his godhood and to carry through the processes of soul growth. In so doing we overlook the spiritual potential, the true light that lives within us each, which light has the capacity to transfigure and redeem the Earth, not so much from sin but from separation, from all the elements inherent within matter expression, matter evolution, which create the tensions of multiplicity, of division and of separation. Quite literally that level exists in man which responded to the call of evolution, to the call of lesser lives inherent and living within form, and moved in to be the redeeming bridge, the bridge between all the lesser kingdoms of evolution and the wholeness, the bridge between matter and energy, the bridge between spirit and form.

Those of the palace of paradise who did not descend are those beings who are largely upon the evolutionary path of the devas and the angelic forms. Man represents a spiritual being, initially at one with the devas, who descended, who actually renounced his oneness and moved into form in order that he would be in a position to redeem form, to lift it up through understanding,

74

through attunement, through seeing clearly what is behind form.

It is very interesting that the queen, who is Buddha's mother, Siddartha's mother, is named Maya which is also the term for illusion, the creator of the sense world. There is a great deal of symbolism in Buddha's life: the being born through or into illusion, and through the clear perception of his consciousness dispelling it, seeing the reality behind form and through that seeing becoming one with it, and through that at-one-ment releasing an energy upliftment.

As we enter into the New Age what we are entering into is a cycle, a period of time, a period of unfoldment when that represented by Buddha, that represented by Christ, that represented by Krishna when he speaks of himself moving in from age to age, to give help to the weak and to restore the law, that oneness which divides itself and then returns to one.

Man is also that same spirit. He is that presence and the glory and promise of this age. Its meaning as a new age is that for the first time in human history we have a chance to take up a conscious, creative recognition of this fact and begin acting upon it. Up to this time we have moved with evolution. Now comes the time to become the servants of evolution and through our own consciousness, through that which we have individually and collectively, to release the light, the love, the wisdom that will bring our renunciation of spiritual estate to its fruition, in the occult redemption of the world.

The Christ

Humanity is the world initiate, the world saviour, and ultimately it is upon the shoulders of humanity that the future and the translation for the entry into light of this planet rest.

Mankind, in order to reach that destiny has travelled an interesting path. When he entered into physical embodiment as a racial idea, not as individuals but as the whole racial consciousness that we call humanity many many millennia ago, he became subject to what can best be described as the will of God acting through nature. He was a being or more appropriately a creature completely ruled by the group consciousness of the natural world, and particularly as that group consciousness expressed itself through instinct. Indeed various instincts were deliberately implanted into man by the overlighting spiritual consciousnesses that governed his evolution so that he might develop in the proper fashion.

In time the human race passed through a great process which kindled in the race, but not necessarily in individuals, the quality that we call mind; and it was at this time when mind first flamed out within the race of man that the spiritual Hierarchy came into existence, although at that time it was composed almost entirely of beings from other evolutionary paths.

When I say that mind came to the race of man and not to individuals, I mean it is just like in a fire; you are going to get some pieces of fuel to burn with greater rapidity and greater light than do others. Some pieces of coal that get out into the side of the fire may not even burn at all, or burn very lightly. There has always been a vast difference in the manifestation of any quality when it is considered on an individual level. There is no such thing as equality of expression though there is equality of source. We all derive from the same divine source, and have the same divine potentials.

Certain beings within the race of humanity progressed very, very rapidly. One such being had achieved a position of mastership at a time when humanity as a whole was still in its infancy; and this being travelled a path which in the Orient would be called the path of the Bodhisattva. A Bodhisattva is a being who has earned the right to enter into Nirvana or into illumination, but he turns back from that state and does not enter it. Instead he turns his face and his attention back to humanity, back to the other lives that are following after him, and in essence pledges himself not to enter an illumined state until all the lives that are lesser than him can do so as well. He becomes in essence a world server.

The first being of this nature who actually emerged from the human race and did not come from other evolutionary paths of the past is the being who in history has become known as the Christ.

While some individuals were progressing very very rapidly under the stimulation of mind and were passing the early initiations, the mass of humanity was learning what it meant to behave as individuals. They were experiencing for the first time the full impact of the quality that we call free will, and gradually over the centuries man became increasingly aware of himself as an isolated individual.

This is an important and vital step. It is necessary for the fulfilment of man's destiny—whatever that destiny may be in its fullness and no human consciousness is presently aware of it in its fullness—that man free himself from the group consciousness of the will of God as it manifests through nature, or the instinctive consciousness. He had in some way to learn how to prove himself as an individual and not simply be part of the undiscriminating, undiscerning mass of pure reactive consciousness. As a consequence the quality and awareness of self had to develop, and this is primarily developed through the discriminatory faculty of the mind.

In Christian symbolism, and in Judaic symbolism, it is said that man ate of the fruit of the tree of knowledge of good and evil, and as a consequence was banished from Eden. This is considered a fall, but esoterically it is not considered so. As man began to develop his faculties of will and his faculties of self-hood, there were naturally set forth for him various precepts and patterns which he should follow and obey in order to use this energy for the greatest good of the whole. But actually one of the faculties, one of the necessary experiences of learning to be a free agent, a free self, is to be able to choose whether one wishes to obey or not; and many individuals, in fact most individuals, within the human race began to express and to create according to the emotional, mental, physical patterns as they were evident to him through his sensory and psychic mechanism.

The ultimate result of this was the creation upon the planet of various powerful thought-forms by a relatively few individuals who had progressed fairly rapidly, but had progressed rapidly in terms of what we would call selfishness, or extreme awareness of self-hood, and had not balanced this with an equal awareness of the greater whole. It was the existence of these thought-forms and all that they invoked, drawing upon energies which man should have been leaving behind: energies of the past; energies of his animal nature, but now given a potency and a vibrancy which no animal consciousness could ever give to them therefore they were truly monstrous, they were unnatural; and energies drawn from sources of the involutionary arc, the arc of descendant matter.

The end result of all this was the accumulation upon the inner realms of the planet of a vast host of what in psychological terms would be called neuroses. Energy which had become bound and could no longer circulate properly was no longer part of the cycle of life, but was simply like a knot to pressure and tension exerting itself upon the mass unconscious of the race, just as buried memories and patterns may exert influences upon the subconscious of an individual.

All energy is living. In fact energy and life are two synonymous terms. And thought-forms of this nature, though not immortal, nevertheless possess a rather primitive form of life, an elemental life, which like most life at that level seeks to preserve itself. It seeks to maintain itself and to keep its form intact forever if it could. As a consequence these thought-forms, possessing such vital energy as they have been able to draw from the race of man, have preyed like parasites upon the race of man in order to maintain themselves in existence. It is the creation and the ultimate effects of this pattern of mass racial neuroses which can best be described by the fall.

Let us return to the concept of the Christ. What is the Christ? Within all life there exists a quality, an energy, which has as its basic characteristic irresistible growth, irresistible and inevitable expression of divinity. It is a quality which says that whatever form I am encased in I will not be held prisoner by that form, but I will transform it into a greater form. I will use all life, all experiences as stepping stones to greater revelations of divinity. The Christ is the basic evolutionary force within creation.

If one uses the geometric symbolism of the triangle with the father, the mother, the male, the female, the positive, the negative polarities, which interacting create a third, it is the third which holds the reality, the tension, the energy, the potential inherent in the relationship. Quite literally, the energy that is the Christ is that life, love, intelligence, energetic power which maintains all creation in existence. It is within each one of us.

On an individual level it is essentially the presence of the Christ that inspires in us discontent, dissatisfaction with the forms through which we are living and experiencing, and that keeps us moving, keeps us dynamic. On an individual level we can, of course, deny that and encase ourselves in forms, mental, emotional, physical. We can cling to certain ideas, certain beliefs, certain opinions, certain ways of doing things, certain habits, and simply refuse to change. But ultimately the presence of this divine force within us will not be thwarted, and ultimately we will need to change, we will need to grow.

This force exists on all levels of creation, but the way in which it exists on each level differs. The manifestation of the Christ within, say, a gooseberry bush or rose is a different manifestation than that which exists within a human being, but it is there none the less. On a planetary level there emerges from the heart and mind of God that stream of living energy which is the dynamic evolutionary impulse that sees that that planet and all the lives upon it moves from the point of its beginning to the point of its completion as a form and then releases the lives to greater forms, to greater destiny. There is, in other words, a planetary Christ power, which derives its strength and impulse from cosmic sources.

This energy, this presence, is focalized or comes together within, and then radiates out from, an individual. He is the kind of individual that must be understood from a spiritual point of view and not from a purely physical one, because our tendency is to see ourselves as individuals and other individuals as being rather limited beings. The extent of our outreach is generally the extent of our flesh. My skin is the limit of me, and for some people my knowledge and my emotional outreach is the limit of what I consider to be me.

But the Christ is an individual, a being, who quite some time ago lost or moved beyond that aspect of experience which we call the isolated or individualized self, just as did the Buddha. The consciousness of the Christ, the life of this being, is completely planetary in scope. Two thousand-odd years ago this being took incarnation upon the Earth and manifested himself through a human vehicle for the purpose of demonstrating the potentiality inherent within each individual. He was the prototype or the expression of the reality of the Christ consciousness which is inherent in us all, and indeed inherent in all that lives, for it is the very energy and life of consciousness itself.

His life accomplished a number of things, and it is this which has laid the foundation for what we are now calling the New Age. This foundation, I believe, must be understood to some extent if we are to truly understand what is asked of us in this present time in human history.

In the Christian teachings the Christ is seen as a divine being, literally God in incarnation, who came to take upon himself the sins of humanity, and by becoming the scapegoat for humanity he paved the way for our salvation through the shedding of his blood. This is only partially true. It represents a certain interpretation of the Christ life which was grafted on after the fact, because the Jewish dispensation, the dispensation of the age of Aries—and Jesus entered in at the close of the age of Aries which zodically speaking is the age of the lamb, and it manifested itself through the great Judaic religion which taught the concept of the scapegoat, the sacrificial lamb; whereas Christ is the messiah or the avatar at the time of the Piscean age who is symbolized by the fish.

Yet what we now think of as the Christ pattern is associated not with the true symbolism of Pisces, but with the symbolism of the preceding age, the scapegoat. Therefore that which Christ is most remembered for is not his life nor indeed his attunement to divinity nor indeed anything that he manifested as representative of the potentials within humanity, but he is best remembered as being a sacrificial lamb.

In essence, what has happened is that the teachings of the Christ were forced back into a mould that was two thousand years more ancient and should have been completed at the time of his first coming. Yet there is some truth to the fact that part of the action of the Christ did accomplish a certain saving effect as far as planetary consciousness went.

For our purposes there are three aspects, three things which the Christ accomplished, which I feel are important. The first is symbolized by Pisces, the fish; the second is symbolized by his being a world saviour, certain energies which he made manifest; and the third is symbolized by his Last Supper. Actually the three stages are the Fish, Gethsemane, and the Last Supper.

What do we mean by the fish? If we take the phrase: Jesus Christ Son of God Saviour, the first letters of that phrase written in Greek form the word that means fish, and throughout early Christian history the fish was always used as a symbol for the little groups of people who would get together and meet in secret, in the days of the Roman Empire when to be a Christian meant death. Christ called his followers and bade them be fishers of men, and in fact most of them were fishermen.

But there was a much deeper meaning than that. The fish is a creature that swims in the midst of the sea and contains within himself the sea. The sea passes in and through the fish, through his gills. He extracts nourishment, oxygen, and so on. The bulk of a fish's body, like the bulk of our body, is water, salt water, sea water.

This is a very appropriate symbolism for man, for individual man. Each of us is a fish moving through the oceans of God, ocean of spirit. The thing that Jesus was trying to demonstrate is this complete attunement of circulation with the wholeness. I breathe it in. I draw it in. I am one with the whole, one with God. It enters my being and it moves out from my being as love, as wisdom, as light, as divine quality. The fish, far more than man, is right there in his living environment. He is surrounded by water everywhere. And so is man. Each of us is contained within a vast spiritual livingness, living presence. This is spoken of in the New Testament as 'He in whom we live and move and have our being.' Jesus was actually asking us to be 'fishers of God,' for that is the realized divine human state: 'I am attuned, I am one with the whole.'

Jesus also demonstrated, manifested, the quality of divinity which we call love. Buddha demonstrated that of wisdom. Jesus demonstrated the blending of the two in love-wisdom. He is known as the great avatar of love. Up to that time, of course God had been referred to from time to time as love, but never with the kind of potency that Jesus actually manifested, or the Christ manifested through him.

Jesus often spoke of this divine human state. He said: 'Be ye perfect even as your Father in heaven is perfect.' He said: 'Greater things than I do, ye shall do.' And he consistently sought to draw man's attention not to himself but to the reality of what was operating through him and within him, because that is the reality inherent in us each.

The second factor that Jesus demonstrated was the Gethsemane experience. This was incredibly potent and perhaps much more significant than it has been given credit for being. The crucifixion and the resurrection, all that happened after the experience in the Garden of Gethsemane, are not of themselves as important for they are simply the physical plane follow-throughs of action taken during the Gethsemane experience, which was the counterpart of the Buddha's great renunciation.

What is the hallmark of the Gethsemane experience? It is expressed in the statement of Jesus: 'Not my will, Father, but thine be done.' There is a power inherent in renunciation and in sacrifice, but it is a power that man has not yet really learned to tap or even to understand, because sacrifice is generally interpreted on human levels as meaning giving something up and is associated with pain and suffering. But if we look at the life of Jesus and of Buddha, we see that in each case what they gave up was hardly anything compared to what followed as a result of that renunciation. And each of us can experience this to some degree when we are faced with an experience in life and through an act of will we overcome a reactive pattern, an emotional pattern, an instinctive physical pattern, a mental pattern which may be moving us in areas that we do not particularly want to go, or which we may know is not for our highest good.

We can give up the good in order to get the best, in other words; and there is a certain power that is released in this, if it is done in the spirit of love and true renunciation and not in any kind of emotional consciousness of martyrdom: 'Oh, I'm so holy because I have given this up and that up and the other thing up!' Renunciation, as Jesus demonstrated it, is the release of the human will to the divine will.

Now this release goes far and away beyond simple obedience. In Eastern philosophy, the image is expressed of the droplet that returns to the ocean and merges with the ocean; but in point of fact the expression of the greater consciousness, of the Christ consciousness, or the Nirvana consciousness, can be more appropriately described as the ocean entering the drop, because the individual in releasing himself and surrendering himself in no way is lost but suddenly finds himself in an even greater capacity and even greater potentiality than was previously possible.

Again the Christ has said: 'Where man would find himself, he must lose himself.' Almost all really successful people have experienced this in their life. In some way they have lost themselves in something that was greater than their immediate vision and desire, and by so doing they have re-found their meaning within an area of much greater vision and desire and of motivation. The reason I said that this goes beyond simple obedience is that you do not really obey yourself. When you are aware of your motivations and follow them, you are being yourself. When you are one with the will of God you are simply being yourself to an even greater degree, a much more transcendent extent.

Up to the time of Jesus the divine will, the actual energy of will had not been really anchored or manifested within the consciousness of humanity. As a consequence the various thought-form patterns that had been created through the exercise of individual human wills had really not much to counteract them. But with the Gethsemane experience and other patterns in Jesus' life, the Christ was able to actually anchor within the realm and sphere of human potentiality the ability to tune in and manifest the divine will. In point of fact, the energy and life of the Christ entered into and became part of the life of the planet, and added new power, new potency, new life, new light, to the life of the planet. This made it possible for all lives within Earth's influence, including your life and my life, to be able to draw upon that increased potency and therefore by drawing it in like a fish draws in nourishment from the ocean, an ocean now greatly vitalized and enriched, to confront the neuroses of past experience and to transform them, to heal them; to confront the karmic weight and burden that human thought patterns and feeling patterns had created, and to literally transmute them.

Christ demonstrated a quality of divine consciousness that up to that time had been little understood because in both the dispensation of Buddha and in the Judaic teachings the emphasis was on the operation of law through wisdom. (If you do this, this will result. If you do A, you will get A-prime. If you do B, you will get B-prime. If you plant corn seed, you will get corn, and so on.) The thing that Christ demonstrated and made manifest and which is very dimly expressed through the doctrine of the sacrificial lamb, is the divine quality of grace, which is really nothing more than the operation of divine will transcending the operation of cause and effect on the level of human will.

It is this power that has made it possible through the past two thousand years for humanity to really confront the products of its past negative creativity (it has created much that is positive as well, but here we are concerned with past negative creativity) and throw it off. Man has literally been able to draw to his aid, in ways never before possible, the power of the divine through learning how even to the most minute degree to renounce his isolated creativity and will in order that he can expand into the greater creativity and will of the Beloved.

The New Age, as we are now experiencing it, would not be possible if this had not occurred. This was a true turning point in the evolution of the planet and released for us a presence of divinity which we can draw to ourselves and express to greatly accelerate and enhance the unfoldment of our divinity. The best example I can give to this is, like here at Findhorn, if we planted a seed within the soil as it previously existed, that seed might germinate and grow but it would be a rather scraggly thing and it might take a long time. But by adding love, light and compost, and more compost, and more love and light, and other things, we create an environment in which that seed can unfold more rapidly, with greater vigour, greater size, with greater life than would have been otherwise possible. So in essence Jesus added compost to this soil of Earth. He enriched the subtler planes of the planet and made the evolutionary power of the Christ more accessible to all that lives.

The third factor is that contained within the Last Supper, and is also contained within a statement that Jesus made when he was preparing to leave, when he said: 'Where two or more are gathered together in my name, there am I.' You will remember from the Bible story in the New Testament that Jesus bade his disciples to go into Jerusalem and to find a man bearing a water pitcher, to follow him to the upper room and there the communion would be celebrated. The New Age is the age of communication, of communion, communion on three levels: man to man, as manifested by right and wholesome human relations (by wholesome I mean relations that create and reveal the wholeness between us); man to Nature, man's oneness with all the lives of earth, animal, vegetable, mineral; and man to spirit, man's oneness with the more evolved life forms such as the Christ and the Hierarchy, and man's oneness with God. So there can be demonstrated the reality of one humanity, one planet, and indeed one life.

The man bearing the water pitcher, as has been stated innumerable times in the past ten years, is the same symbol as the zodiacal sign of Aquarius. We are indeed entering the sign of Aquarius. So Jesus was illustrating the fact that much of his work was preparatory, laying the foundations for the greater work which the Christ can take up and make manifest in this age, when he again reappears as the Aquarian avatar. For now humanity as a whole is in a far greater state, much more able to respond to his message, respond to the energies of love, of wisdom, of divine will, than humanity could have responded two thousand years ago.

This is also illustrated in the fact that it is no longer through the isolated individual, the fish, that the divine revelation is coming. It is through that which reveals and pours out the life and splendour of the divine, and Jesus gave the key to this when he said: 'When two or more are gathered together in my name, there is the Christ.' Again I should say the Christ gave the key to this. We come into the age of the group again. We have come full cycle, moving from the group consciousness of nature through the self-hood of man where man learns to be, to recognize and to be his own divine centre, and now in the next two thousand years or so man learns how to blend his divine centre in wholeness, in cooperation with the will of the Beloved not as an external force but as that which is revealed through the communion and communication of the whole. Jesus, again the Christ, is revealed when we come together. In the interaction of two people in relationship, the Christ is either made manifest or he is not made manifest, depending on whether that relationship manifests wholeness or whether it increases separation.

From twos and threes and fours and fives we build towards a world of several million souls, indeed billions of souls, all of whom can be meshed together in time in the vast communion of life. It is only when that is accomplished and all lives share in this flow of oneness that we can say that the Christ revelation initiated two thousand years ago will have completed itself.

Perhaps at that time more and different and certainly far greater revelations of the nature and manifestation of divinity will come, and we will have deeper insights into the nature of God and our relationship with that centre, with that source. But this is possible for us because of the work, the life, the energies anchored by the great beings of the past and particularly Buddha and the Christ who more or less summed it all up. Within their teachings lie all the keys that we need to enter the New Age: the Four Noble Truths of the Buddha, the Eightfold Path of balance, of discrimination, discernment, wisdom; the life of love, of service, of unity, of wholeness, of attunement and realization of divinity which the Christ made manifest.

The New Age is not really all that new. It is the continuation of vast programmes of spiritual and evolutionary development initiated ages ago, but perhaps it will have some new surprises as well.

Whether it will or not can be determined in future revelations, not necessarily same time, same channel. But somewhere each of us within the beginning of this new cycle will find revelations of the divine beyond that which has previously come to man. These revelations more than ever before will emerge from humanity, for now humanity is finally at the stage, having been brought to this point by the work of the Buddha and the Christ, where it can take up its role as being a world initiate.

Chapter
seven

The Foundation of Ritual

One of the reasons that we say that we are moving into a new age is because of the cyclic manifestation of energy within nature. In this sense we are referring to cosmic nature and not just planetary nature. For the past twenty-five hundred years or so the Earth has been largely influenced by a certain quality of energy which is now phasing out, and it is being replaced by another which occultly is called the energy of the Seventh Ray. It is this energy which will become for the duration of this new cycle the dominant, qualifying, or characterizing force operating through planetary civilization, not just human civilization but that of Nature and all of its kingdoms as well.

The Seventh Ray has been called in occult history the ray of ceremonial magic, the ray of ritual. Since our lives and our civilization and our spiritual development are going to be to a great extent conditioned by this energy for the next twenty-five hundred years, it is good in understanding the vision of the New Age to have an understanding of what the Seventh Ray implies and what it is going to create in our world. In order to have this understanding we need to clarify what is meant by ritual.

When one talks about ceremonial magic the average individual will almost surely think of the magician, of ceremony, of a man or a woman dressed in robes doing something, often doing things which the public imagination is quite aghast at and yet terribly interested in at the same time;

working in strange hide-aways with exotic and esoteric diagrams on the floor and using strange implements. Certainly this image has existed, has been real in the past, and for that matter it still is. One of the minor manifestations of the incoming ray is a resurgence of interest in all forms of magic, black and white, and in ceremony in general. This is largely augmented by the fact that there are an awful lot of people who have been magicians in the past who are taking incarnation now, attempting to recapitulate their patterns.

If this is our image of ritual and of magic, then we shall probably come up with some unique and exotic conceptions of what the new civilization is going to be like, conceptions which will be entirely wrong. So let us go a little deeper into this.

There is not one thing that exists in the physical realm which has been brought into manifestation without ritual. Ritual is the creative means by which everything of which we are aware comes into our awareness and takes form. The Seventh Ray is more accurately known as the ray of manifestation, of ordered activity and of communication. All life, all form, all manifestation of energy are based on ritualistic expression, if by ritual we mean activity which has an order, a rhythm, a harmony, and the quality of inter-relationship about itself.

For example, a basic ritual on which all organic life on Earth depends is the ritual of the food cycle that moves through the plant kingdom. The plant has the remarkable ability of actually capturing free energy and trapping it within highly complex organic molecules. It does this by receiving sunlight which in the presence of chlorophyll is used to catalyze the building up of highly complex molecules from very simple ones which the plants draw from the air and from the soil. These highly complex molecules then provide food for more highly developed organisms like animals, and for the plant itself. When an animal eats plant tissue or animal tissue, these highly complex molecules are broken down through the processes of digestion and energy is released. It is this release of energy that allows organic life as we know it to take place. The cycle is brought to completion by the creation of waste material: carbon dioxide from respiration, which the plant then inhales; and solid and liquid waste from the body including the bodies themselves when death occurs, which are then reduced to basic simple organic and inorganic molecules by the process of decay.

This is an incredible and beautiful cycle if you think about it and it is very simple. The food chain is quite simple to diagram and yet very complex in all of its parts. Its success depends upon the cooperation and the harmony of a great number of organisms and a great number of systems of energy. One of the arguments that is being used at the present time to illustrate the concept that man is an endangered species is based on this complexity of the inter-dependency of the web of life, and it revolves around pollution of the oceans. One may think that the oceans could absorb a great deal of waste, but one of the most important aspects of the ocean is the microscopic life that lives close to the shore and is largely responsible for the production of oxygen in the planet. It is this life which is easily poisoned by the introduction of chemical waste, D.D.T. for example, into the ocean carried down through river beds. Those scientists who are interested in this kind of research state that it would not take a great deal of pollution, really very little, to wipe out enough of these micro-organisms to irreversibly destroy the oxygen-producing cycle of the planet. This would mean that by destroying something that is so small that we cannot see it, we destroy the ability of the Earth to generate oxygen. That means we destroy ourselves.

The inter-relatedness of life is so tightly woven together that it takes a very unaware being to persist in saying that his or her actions are entirely his or her own business and have no relatedness to other life forms upon the planet. Whether or not the ecologists are correct in their doom predictions is another matter; but they are bringing forcefully into public and mass awareness the concept of the inter-relatedness of life: the fact that there is no action which a person can take which does not have repercussions throughout the entire web of the planet. It is also portraying very beautifully the rituals on which planetary life is based. For this is a ritual—a ritual characterized by rhythm, which means moving cyclicly through time: inbreaths, outbreaths; periods of quiescence, periods of activity; periods of life, periods of death—a ritual as characterized by communication, parts relating together in such a way that energy is exchanged between them. It is characterized by harmony. In general it is characterized by the existence of ordered cooperative activity.

When man began to become aware in a religious sense a millenium ago, one of the ways in which he was taught was through the medium of ritual. Rituals were created for him by more advanced consciousnesses in order that he might participate in—actually enter in as if into a drama—certain of the great natural rituals and have them more forcefully implanted into his consciousness. An example of this is the dervish dance of the Sufi, in which the dancers all perform as if they were planetary bodies moving in space, the whirling motion and the circular motion which the dancers follow are all very closely calculated to represent the movement of the planets around the Sun, the movement of the planets around their own axis and so forth. All of which generates energy. We know that the movement of the Earth around its axis generates night and day. We know that the movement of the Earth around the Sun generates the seasons, as well as the tilting of the Earth on its axis. If it were not for these cycles, life as we know it would not exist. Ritual is by no means a static manifestation. It is highly dynamic, it is the manifestation of energy in motion, but moving not in a chaotic random way but in an ordered pattern.

Man in the early days of his existence as a thinking being was instructed how to participate in large ritual ceremonies, so that he would then have the experience of invoking various energies which otherwise are contacted more abstractly through Nature, like the energy of the Sun, the energy of the Earth in its motion, the energy of the seasons, energies of life and death. In time, however, ritual itself came to be seen as practically an end in itself, rather than as a teaching form. It is also true that during the centuries when the Seventh Ray was not in dominant manifestation one of the ways in which the energy of that ray could be invoked was through ordered activity.

Think about this for just a moment. In order for anything to happen on the physical level, there has to be some element of coordination occurring. Some kind of organization has to exist. If I want to move, or if I wish to speak, then various parts of my body have to engage in a ritual of cooperation. There has to be some communication between my intent, my brain, my muscles. If that is not present, then I am unable to function as a physical being. My energies dissipate themselves randomly.

Ceremonial magic used to be the science of humanity. Rather elaborate rituals were established which, through the medium of creating an ordered environment, energies moving in certain definite patterns through the relationship of people—a man chanting certain sounds, other men moving in certain patterns, geometrical patterns and so on—all created within their consciousness a sense of order.

Patterns themselves are not that important. Magic does not operate on a physical level. Magic is purely psychological and the ritual is designed to create a psychological state. But that state in me combined with that state in others provides a highly cooperative foundation through which energy can be channelled; and once that energy is channelled it can be used to do work. That is strictly what magic is. Magic is a way of transferring energy from one level to another for the purpose of doing work, for the purpose of effecting a change.

With that kind of a definition we realize that just about everything that we do is magic, magical. It is also true that in the early days of man's development it was within the temple structures that organization reached its highest peak and the sciences of government, the sciences of cooperative activity, the sciences of human relations were taught and were known in their highest extent. That is why the rulers of the ancient countries all had to be graduates of the temples. Only a person who had experienced this had the knowledge of how to so order a mass of the people within the country that certain definite results could be obtained.

It was through various ritualistic experiences, and organizations that were cultivating such experiences, that early humanity was trained in how to work effectively with physical plane energy. The Seventh Ray controls physical plane manifestation.

As man developed, however, this need for ritual has become less and less, and correspondingly rituals have tended to become more and more static. People go through the motions without really knowing what they are doing or why. Of course that destroys the psychological state on which the effectiveness of any ritual depends, until we come to our age when we are in a position to recognize to a far greater degree the reality of organization and of coordinated activity. In fact our society cannot exist without it and that will be increasingly true in the age that is ahead.

Interestingly enough many futurist individuals who attempt to project into the future—I do not mean by this prophets in a psychic sense but prophets in an economic or a political or a sociological sense—play around with the idea of the future human state being roughly equivalent to that of a highly organized beehive or ant hill. A number of novels, science fiction novels and movies, have been produced to this effect, one of the earliest being *Nineteen Eighty-Four* by George Orwell. *Brave New World* by Aldous Huxley was one and there are a number of others. The reason that this is interesting is that what these people are tuning into is a definite Seventh Ray manifestation but seen through the eyes of a person who is still attuned to the preceding cycle which emphasized the surrendering of self to a greater cause—devotion in other words and idealism. If you put these two together, what you are most likely to come up with is the concept of the highly organized state which is all important, and the individual who must be devotionally surrendered to the state.

This does not in any way express the true intent of the Seventh Ray, which is completely dependent upon the existence of strongly motivated, highly intelligent and free individuals. The energy of cooperative activity can only be released when there is only cooperative activity; and cooperative activity is based not on coercion but on the free giving of one's self through love and understanding that a greater whole may be made manifest. When we talk about working for the good of the whole we are talking under the influence of the Seventh Ray. When we talk about surrender to the whole we may be talking under the influence of the ray that is going out and therefore we may be talking in retrogressive terms.

The Seventh Ray demands or depends for its successful manifestation on the existence of fulfilled individuals. A true ritual is made up of the whole system, the dynamic system and the individual units operating within that system, in this case human beings. Both are important: the system nourishes the units and the units nourish the system and both are required in balance together. Therefore the concept of individual freedom, the concept of liberation, the concept of release from encasing forms, from static states, is also very much a Seventh Ray impulse.

Man's early rituals were drawn from the cycles and rituals which he saw in Nature. In time man became aware of the processes, the ritualistic processes occurring within his own consciousness. In time to come these will determine the rituals of his future. For example, modern business corporations and the modern economic world, particularly in the capitalistic countries, tend very much towards Seventh Ray manifestation. The highly successful business man and financier is a good prototype of a Seventh Ray individual. Of course he can be functioning positively or negatively, can be expressing the impulse selfishly for power or he can be doing it for the good of the greater whole; but the business world, economic world, is tightly interlocked in a very ritualistic sense. When for instance imbalances in trade-flows made it necessary for Britain to float its currency, the floating of the pound created repercussions throughout the entire economic world. All countries had to adjust in some way. This sense of one action taking place in one part of a system affecting the entire system and therefore altering the way in which it manifests is a Seventh Ray experience.

Findhorn in its seeking to establish a community based on people working together, freely working together for the good of the whole, communicating together, fitting in together, and the emphasis here on organization, on order, is an expression of Seventh Ray activity. No true ritual can manifest in the presence of chaos. The function of a ritual is to translate chaos into order so that energy can flow freely, powerfully, and not be dissipated. The function of all rituals in Nature is either to transfer energy from one state to another, like from the plant to an animal in the sense of food, or to translate it from one level to another, as for example energy into matter which the plant performs, or matter back into energy which the atomic bomb performs.

The Seventh Ray is very much the ray of transference, of movement. It is the ray which comes into play whenever any individual takes incarnation, because it is the ray that must be used to build up the body. It is the gateway into physical form. If your body were to assemble randomly, if anything disrupts the ordered manifestation of the development of your body, you may not live. So in understanding the Seventh Ray we need to see it far beyond the boundaries of the terms that have up to this point been used to express it. The characteristics of the Seventh Ray in the past have largely been demonstrated, it is true, by people who have worked deliberately with ceremony and ritual to invoke various energies. Hence it has become known as the ray of ceremonial magic. But if the true meaning of magic and of ritual is understood, we are in a position to grasp what is happening now within our society and our culture and what is going to happen. The Seventh Ray is basically the ray that manifests all the qualities of organization, of cooperative activity, of communication, of inter-relationship on a physical level, and physical energy which make possible that phenomenon that we call civilization.

The incoming of this ray is going to have many interesting effects. It is with these effects as they are known or can be known at the present time, and some of the impacts upon our consciousness, that I shall deal in the next chapter. It is sufficient now that we ground ourselves with a broader realization of what this ray implies, what it has implied in the past, and what its role is in a cosmic sense. It is the building ray, but it is also the ray of destruction, because all builders are also destroyers. To build something you generally have to destroy something that was there first in order to clear room for it, and to release the energy that has been trapped in static form. Man-made rituals, which tend to be organized either emotionally or by the mind, have a tendency to fall into a static state. The presence of the Seventh Ray rather than enhancing ritual magic will tend to destroy it, and rather than seeing an increase in magic of the kind that has been practised in the past, an increase of wizards and magicians upon the Earth, we will see a decrease.

But a new kind of magician will take their place. In some ways he has already appeared and his work has been largely negative; that is it has been used in a negative fashion. But it can be highly positive once we learn to understand it. This magician is very ably portrayed by the advertising executive, because all forms of advertising are a form of ritual magic but using now a ritual understanding of psychological energy in order to produce results, to stimulate desire, to stimulate thinking along certain lines and to order thinking along certain lines. All forms of propaganda are a subtle blend of Seventh Ray energy and the energies of education and wisdom. Advertising as it has evolved in the past thirty years is one of the forerunners of the new magic of Seventh Ray expression. It has been used to control, to influence rather than to communicate and to communicate in such a way that people are made free.

If you think about it advertising is definitely a ritual. There are very few things, even refrigerators or automobiles, that are sold today without at least one bathing beauty in the picture with as few clothes as the culture will permit. Not because the refrigerator is particularly useful to a bathing beauty, in fact it may be rather unpleasant to sit in a refrigerator with just a bikini on, but because knowing the psychology of the masses, or at least thinking that they do, it is known that certain images will stimulate certain responses which by train of association become projected onto other things which are entirely unrelated. So suddenly the refrigerator becomes sexy, or a given product becomes sexy, and therefore it has greater appeal.

The Seventh Ray is intimately associated with the Kundalini. The lord of the Seventh Ray—by which I do not mean the human lord within the Hierarchy, the Master Rakoczi, but the actual being, the cosmic being, who is

100

the personification of the Seventh Ray—controls the flow of energy from the Sun to the planet, and it is this flow of energy which is the cosmic equivalent of Kundalini. As a consequence the Seventh Ray is intimately associated with the sexual function and with sexual energy, creative energy which is sexual on many levels, not just on the physical level. It is interesting to see how as this ray swings into motion we are increasingly coming into greater and greater confrontation with the question of sex and sexual relations within humanity; also with the use of sexual stimuli to motivate people, to get them to purchase things, to consume things.

It is being done on a large scale, but it is exactly what was done in the ancient rituals when the Kundalini force was invoked through the man or the woman or both, in order to contact various elemental forces and get them to do things. Sexual magic is the oldest form of magic known to man, because it has such a close relationship to the Seventh Ray and expresses its power on the physical level. Man has always been interested in doing things physically rather than spiritually.

As this ray comes into play we see these vast rituals becoming externalized on a mass scale, and we see the new magic, the new ceremony coming into being. Whether this will characterize the New Age or not is another question. It is far more likely that we are witnessing simply a transitional use of the impulse of the Seventh Ray.

Chapter eight

The Seventh Ray

It is very important that we see and know what is happening in our world, not only in planetary terms but in personal terms. The New Age vision is not a great scheme which is being worked out which we can observe, like we observe things on the television. The New Age is not only a planetary or a cosmic occurrence but it is very much a personal one. Some of the information which I am sharing with you may seem to have little personal relevance. I am dealing with things which must be expressed in the widest possible terminology. But the meaning behind all these things is very definitely an individual meaning.

It is not my objective to give you a lot of esoteric or occult information about the Seventh Ray. The Tibetan master, Djwal Khul, who has set forth perhaps the most complete exposition of the rays, has done so in something like forty thousand pages of material. So if anyone wishes to go into the matter in some detail, it is there for you. My aim is to relate what information has been given about the Seventh Ray with what is happening to us as individuals and what our role must be.

What do we mean when we talk about the Seventh Ray? What is a ray? The name seems to imply something like a beam of energy, like you get from a spotlight. It also implies that there are seven of them and we are talking about the seventh one. In actual fact we are dealing with one of the concepts that lie behind creation as we know creation in this solar system, in which the lord of the solar system, the great being who is by far and away the most evolved being that any of us can possibly have contact with at the present time in human evolution, created this slice of the universe through a process that is best described as the utterance of a word, the sounding of a note, the sending forth of a vibration, which encompassed within itself all the dreams and visions and hopes and ideals and plans, if they may be referred to as such, which this great being had as his objectives in creating the solar system in the first place. This word had seven syllables; or to put it another way, there were seven emanations from the heart and mind of God, the seven spirits before the throne, seven archangels, and each of these emanations is itself a manifestation of an aspect, or an idea, or a particular kind of divine activity.

There are three primary rays and four subsidiary ones. The three primary ones are: first, the energy of will or divine creativity; the second is the energy of love and wisdom or divine life; and the third is the energy of intelligence or divine mind.

Following these three under the manifestation of divine mind are four ways in which the mind functions—and my words may be a bit misleading but they are the best that we can do at the present time. One is through consideration of the objective meaning behind form, which is called the Fifth Ray and it has its manifestation in what we call science. There is the use of mind in the formulation of ideals and in generating a certain energy of devotionalism; this is the Sixth Ray. The Christian religion and the Islamic religion are the two greatest manifestations of a Sixth Ray consciousness, devotion to a particular type or a form or a person. The Seventh Ray is the ray of ordered activity, but it is also a good deal more.

Between the three primary and the three subsidiary rays is another one which seeks to blend the two of them together and it is often called the ray of harmony through conflict; the creation of balance through the resolution of the opposites. It is the ray of beauty and of harmony and is called the Fourth Ray. In any event all seven of these rays represent seven manifestations from the one source consciousness, and each of these rays is itself a living being. The term 'ray' is somewhat misleading. A ray is the manifestation of the quality and consciousness of a living being. It is a kind of life which is very much beyond any life which we are going to encounter as long as we reside in physical form.

Everything that is created is created through the mutual interaction of these seven beings. That is why they are called in religious and esoteric literature the seven builders. But the Seventh Ray is more than any, as far as the physical plane is concerned, the ray of building. It is the ray of the physical plane and everything that we see in physical form exists because of the operation of the Seventh Ray. The Seventh Ray orders things, it brings things into relationship. Chaos is the absence of relationship, and order is the presence of relationship, particularly relationship which contributes to each other. I contribute to you, you contribute to me; we work together in harmony, we work together in coordination and cooperation and in communication. Until recently the most obvious form of Seventh Ray which we could see is found in the mineral world, particularly through crystalline structures, for the Seventh Ray seeks to make things relate in geometric patterns. But now man has evolved to a point where he is asked to manifest in his relationships the quality of the Seventh Ray; and that is what the New Age is all about.

In any given time cycle upon the Earth one ray is dominant. It is not only one that is functioning—all seven function to some degree—but one is dominant and now we are coming to the time when the seventh is dominant. The impact of this on human consciousness is first of all of a destructive nature, simply because any ray that is building is also a ray of destruction. When the time came for Findhorn to expand and for the terrain on which it is built to be transformed, work had to be done to literally destroy the forms that had existed previously. In some way the terrain is altered, even if only tearing up the wild plants that existed in order to make room for the foundations of buildings; and then the building force can enter and re-form what was present to create new structures.

In human society at the present time we are in a transitional phase which is characterized by the Sixth Ray, or the sixth manifestation of energy; which in turn is generally characterized by an emotional tie to given forms, which we call devotion. An effect of this is to create within the human consciousness a certain quality of attachment. I am attached to the things to which I am devoted. This manifests itself in loyalty to one's ideal of an individual, an image of a spiritual being, a master, or a given church or a given nation or a country; and one of the negative side effects of devotionalism is that it is highly separative. It does not have to be, but it is generally worked out as such.

One of the best recent examples of this, where this country is concerned, is happening right now in Northern Ireland where there is conflict between the devotees of Catholicism and the devotees of Protestantism. The problem with the devotional consciousness is that it tends to focus the person towards a given thought-form or a given institution, but to focus them in an emotional way. One of the characteristics of the emotional plane is that it is divisive. It operates under the law of attraction and repulsion, attracted to some things and repelled from others. This creates a tendency towards a very static state and a lack of communication. The only way in which Protestants and Catholics are communicating in certain parts of Northern Ireland is through bullets. A person who is devoted to an ideal tends to be very rigid. He stays with that ideal until a stronger force moves him from it.

But a characteristic of the Seventh Ray is adaptability, rhythmic relationships, not static ones. It is the ability to be fluid in one's capacity to form relationships with others and with one's environment. It means that if you believe in Buddha, and you believe in Krishna, and you believe in Mohammed, and I believe in Christ, and yet there is a work that we have to do together, we can do it together in full harmony and cooperation and communication.

The Seventh Ray is the ray which makes possible the union between life and matter. It was the ray that was brought into activity when this planet was created, and made possible the entry of spirit into form. Consequently it is the ray of birth, and the Seventh Ray comes into activity with every soul when it takes birth, because it is through the operation of this ray that it is made possible for the soul to take possession of its physical form. It is the ray that links polarities together and makes them work together. Where a human being is concerned it links the form aspect of the consciousness, which is the personality, with the spiritual aspect, which is the soul; and that linking when it is first established creates what is esoterically called the birth of the Christ within.

This is very important because we are told that the New Age is a time when great masses of humanity will experience the birth of the Christ consciousness. We are told that the second coming of the Christ in our age will be fundamentally, most importantly, a mass coming. It will be the manifestation of a consciousness within the multitudes. All of humanity is on the brink of initiation, an initiation into the beginnings of Christ consciousness, which in turn is characterized by compassion, by love, by wisdom, by universal outlook, by the ability to function as part of a group rather than to function as a separated individual.

It is because this is the time in the history of the planet for this to occur that the Seventh Ray or this great being is coming into operation to make it possible. It is through the impact of this ray form within human consciousness that the soul becomes linked to the personality; and through that linking the rhythm of the soul, the rhythm of the higher nature, the rhythm of the Christ consciousness slowly begins to take precedence over the rhythms of the reactive mind and heart, the personality consciousness that simply responds to environmental stimuli and to internal pressures.

Men now cry for freedom. They have cried for it for a long time. Certainly in our age there is a great longing and a great struggle going on within human consciousness for the existence of the quality of freedom. But true freedom does not exist except where the individual is linked with the rhythm of his soul, for it is only from the strength of that centre that he can cope with the rather powerful forces that move through the physical and emotional and mental realms. It is really like saying that we have all been swimming in an ocean and the force of the ocean is greater than any of our individual strengths. We can go with the currents; we can try and swim against them; we can try and go at a tangent to them; but the ocean is always stronger than we are. Suddenly we come across a platform rising from the ocean which is rooted deep into the ocean bed and is absolutely immovable. When we climb up on to that, the currents of the ocean may move about us and the waves may slam against us but we are immovable. That platform is the soul where human life is concerned, for the soul is in no way conditioned by experience in the three worlds of mind, emotion and form—that is, it is not forced into reactivity. It may draw wisdom from its experiences in these worlds, but it is not forced into action.

What will this mean where humanity is concerned? What does the birth of the Christ mean? It will undoubtedly mean a good deal more than we can at present give words to, because so much of the inner life must be experienced before you can even begin to verbalize it or to communicate it with another person. Yet surely the birth of this consciousness means the breaking down of all the thought patterns and energy forms which contribute towards divisiveness and self-orientation.

One of the great challenges at the present time in human affairs is the challenge of nourishment. We live in a world in which a very small percentage of the world's population occupying a few countries, primarily two or three or four, consume something like seventy to eighty per cent of the world's resources and nourishment. Something like eighty per cent of the world's population is consuming the other twenty per cent. This condition of imbalance both ecologically and politically will only lead, if uncorrected, to unmitigated and unqualified disaster. What is required is an awareness on the part of individuals that opens them not towards pulling things into themselves for their own use alone, but towards giving, sharing, managing resources, using the many gifts of the planet for the good of the whole planet, of all humanity.

This kind of thing has been talked about for a long time, but within the past decade, in fact within the past five years, the urgency, the sense of something needing to be done and the cultivation of an awareness within human consciousness of the responsibility of the highly industrialized societies to begin to work for the betterment of the developing countries is becoming very much more powerfully part of the forefront of human consciousness. As more and more individuals in the world begin to realize the inter-relatedness of life, the more we will see these principles of inter-relatedness used to bring balance and harmony into political, economic and social relationships. This cannot help but create for us a new civilization.

The Seventh Ray then is the ray of two things: one, it is the ray of birth on the physical level. How many times have we heard Peter and Eileen here say that the function of the New Age is to bring heaven down on Earth! That is a Seventh Ray statement. It is the age in which anyone who seeks to follow the mystical path or the path of the spirit must be very practical and must learn how to draw the resources of that path down into physical form, into some practical, tangible, usable manifestation. Two, it is the ray of ordered activity, of organization. This organization can be very tight but it does not have to be, for the Seventh Ray is the ray of rhythmic relationship and can be very fluid as long as the consciousnesses that are involved are able to deal with this rhythm and not lose their balance and their sense of security. By rhythm I mean that we do not require for our security the existence of static states. For example, I require that I have a guaranteed job through my labour union, because I am afraid that if it is not guaranteed for me I may find myself out of work, and then what will I do? I must see that my institutions are resistant to change, because if they changed, then someway my security is threatened and my relationship to my society is threatened. The keynote of the New Age is the ability to utilize change creatively and not to be frightened by it.

The Seventh Ray is the energy that makes possible the existence of atomic structure and the intricacies of atomic matter; these incredible energy particles that obey no known three dimensional laws, for example particles that can exist in two places at the same time, and particles which are neither particles nor waves of energy but something in between, something that is both yet neither. Yet these remarkable manifestations of energy life relate together. Through that dynamic relatedness they create a state which enables us to experience stability. This chair is very stable. It is not about to suddenly change into a beach ball or a grand piano. It is going to stay just what it is until some outside force alters it. Even then nothing is going to change its atomic structure short of a force that can reach right into the heart of the atom and transmute it.

But all of this manifestation of apparent solidity is highly dynamic motion. Consciousness that is tuned in to the flow and rhythm of life, to what we could call the divine plan, is also capable of that same kind of dynamic relationship and still knowing where it is at. At the present time in our society we have been used to depending upon various definitions in order to assure ourselves of where we are in relationship to that society; and we have seen how man has defined himself and through that definition tends to determine how he will express himself.

What does this mean? Well, we rely on certain labels like teacher, student, follower, parent, child, husband, wife, and all of the various accumulated concepts that encrust these labels; and we tend to insist that we live according to these definitions rather than live according to the reality of life. For example, for years and years the concept of the male, of what was expected of the man, was that he be sexually aggressive, that he be not given to tenderness and emotion, that he be strong, tough; and the woman had to be yielding and soft and given to tears and capable of dropping a hanky at the appropriate moment. People had definitely allowed themselves in Western culture, and other cultures have their own definitions—to order their lives so as to fit these definitions.

This is a subtle manifestation of Sixth Ray energy. It greatly reduces the ability of units to relate and to function in utilizing what could be called the magic of right human relationships, because if I am relating to you as teacher to student, I am not relating to you as David to a group of other people. It is a definition relating to other definitions, rather than a living force relating to other living forces. Naturally I am speaking generally here but we can see how this has worked out in our culture. Because of this, actions which a person may be fully capable of, which yet seem to take them beyond the limits of the given role which they are asked to play, are stifled or at least not understood; and this creates great difficulties when it comes to true communication.

All this is breaking down now, and in the sequence of breaking down we have a great deal of confusion, a lot of experimentation going on. Gradually out of this will return the true order and organization of the Seventh Ray, which is based not on external definition or on form as much as it is based on the energy of consciousness. If I am in touch with my soul, then I know what is right for me and for those with whom my energy comes in contact; and I know it on a far deeper and more powerful level than any moral code or social code or ethical code could ever teach me. Because of this I could in those circumstances relate with individuals as soul to soul and not as form to form.

The Seventh Ray governs the manifestation of the sexual impulse, primarily because that is the impulse that relates life energy through matter on the physical level and is the energy related to birth. Until this ray comes in more fully and the individual's consciousness begin to link up with the soul, experiencing the birth of the Christ within, we are going to see a great deal of confusion and experimentation in the field of sexual and marriage relationships.

Out of all this will emerge the new patterns for the future. These new patterns may not be very much different from what we have had in the past. They may be identical in fact from outward seeming, but they will be incredibly different in terms of the consciousness that lies behind the form.

Each of us is participating in this. We cannot escape it for we are part of the planetary consciousness and we are each moving into this new cycle. We have taken incarnation now, really as part of having a vast privilege; for here we can experience, while in physical embodiment, the initiation of the birth of the Christ. It is possible now for literally hundreds of thousands of people to undergo the first initiation, an event unparalleled in human history, a mass planetary initiation. This I am quite sure is what many of the prophecies are hinting at when they talk about the consciousness being raised to a new dimension, or the Earth suddenly being transformed into light. Out of this emerges a new civilization, because we have new energies to work with—the energy not of the personality to draw upon but the energy of the soul and the cosmic energies upon which the soul can draw new insights, new awareness, new sensitivity.

It is an age in which individual striving is far less important than group aspiration and the ability of the individual to see that. Unlike the Sixth Ray man who fought for the ideal of personal development, which was important in that day and age, we now see the use and value of the personality as an instrument that allows our soul to fulfil its desire and aspiration as part of a group, and the soul is a group consciousness. There is really no such thing as an individualistic soul. It is a contradition in terms. The soul consciousness is the consciousness of that level of awareness of love, of life, which sees only oneness—you and I not necessarily as the same thing but as one thing, one life, one being. Then it becomes a great joy and pleasure to so develop one's self in harmony with the development of the group that the entire group is enhanced, and all benefit.

That which is happening upon the Earth needs to be understood. The Seventh Ray is called the ray of ceremonial magic and ritual. True ritual is the very process of life itself, and what we are coming into is an age when the promise of the Christ can be fulfilled when he said, 'I come to give you life more abundantly.' Surely it is the fulfilment of that which is heralded by the coming of the Christ consciousness to humanity. As man learns to wield the ritual of right human relationships, which is the only true soul magic that there is, he releases into his world more and more energy of life, of creativity, of abundance. He vastly enhances his own individual awareness as the group awareness is enhanced.

The importance of Findhorn is that it is a rather distinct manifestation of the objectives of the Seventh Ray. It is a group community. Its emphasis is upon order and beauty and harmony and it is a place where individuals are exposed to the kind of life which, if understood and worked with, can bring about a link with one's higher nature. In time the kind of consciousness which characterizes this community, not necessarily the exact style that is manifested here but the consciousness that underlies it, will be the consciousness that underlies all of our civilization.

Because we are participants in this we need to understand what is going on and not become caught up in the confusion of the interim period. We need to know what we are working towards so that our life has some direction. We are working towards the ability to communicate beyond prejudice, beyond separation, beyond idealistic divisions with our fellowmen. We are working towards the ability to see clearly what a person is, and not to see them simply in terms of a social role; to relate to them in that fashion and yet to relate to them in such a way that through cooperation, through harmony, through communication, a greater organization is made manifest.

Many people object to the concept of hierarchy, that hierarchy is the natural governing principles of the universe. But one cannot understand hierarchy unless one understands life and sharing and good communication and cooperative interplay through love and awareness and wisdom. Then the true meaning of what a hierarchy is becomes quite clear, not as units stacked on top of units in some vast cosmic pyramid, but lives within lives within lives, all working and communicating together to the benefit of the whole.

Each of us is part of that whole. We are working towards the ability to externalize in our lives the principles which were laid down by Buddha and by the Christ. They are really the foundation stones on which the New Age consciousness rests. For the New Age, as far as humanity goes from the planetary consciousness of the race, is the birth into the Christ consciousness. For some people much higher initiations will be taken. There will be greater consciousnesses unfolding. But the birth of the Christ is the destiny for mass human awareness in this time, and it is towards this that we must work. This is what we must visualize as what is happening now and not be caught up in the apparent confusion and despair of our time period.

The value of knowing about the Seventh Ray lies in the ability of the mind through understanding to dispel the fears and confusions of the emotional level and to begin to grasp what the plan of God is for our time; to begin to work intelligently to further that plan in our lives and in our group experiences. In this way we may serve with a potency far beyond what we may realize. For subtle changes in our being affect not only ourselves but all life upon the planet—mineral, vegetable, animal, human and greater than

114

human. For we are all one. We are all connected.

It will be the destiny of man under the impetus and stimulation of the Seventh Ray to come into the realization of this oneness. It is this realization that will characterize and determine his civilizations for this age onward.

Chapter
nine

The New Age Movement

The history of mankind may very well be expressed as the history of ideas. When an idea catches fire it is like a diamond; many people see different facets of it and respond to these different facets. Quite often each individual or group that has perceived a facet may feel that what it has grasped of the truth is all of the truth, or at least the most fundamental or the most important part of it. If the diamond is not seen in its totality, then fragmentation can occur—a situation not unlike the splintering which happened to the Protestant movement during the late Middle Ages.

Each of us represents a different consciousness, a different quality of the divine brought into manifestation. As we come together in our groups, drawn together because of affinity, our groups likewise represent different aspects. It is important that this is so for the New Age is not a product that can be created the way someone would turn out an automobile or a painting. It is the sum total of the creative expression of many, many lives, not only human lives but angelic, superhuman, subhuman—many levels of consciousness all responding to a divine idea and unfolding to embrace that idea.

The idea of the New Age is not a new one. Many of its characteristics have been discussed in the religions that have preceded our time. In these religions, particularly in the Judaeo-Christian heritage, we find prophecies relating to the end of the age. It is a fact that various individuals—catching the reflection of the divine idea as it moves down into human consciousness and begins to agitate our civilization, begins to break up old forms, creating confusion, creating discontent and creating turmoil—look out upon the civilization responding to these impacts and say: 'These are the latter days.' In fact they have been saying these are the latter days for a little over a thousand years. This is very interesting because the force which is one of the initiators of the New Age civilization did indeed have its entry point into human consciousness a little over a hundred years ago, approximately in the 1820s.

It is interesting to look and see what has happened in that time. We have had the rise of the industrial civilization stimulated as never before. We have had the rise of a number of religious movements which claim to be revelations for the latter days. In America there is a Church of Latter-Day Saints of Jesus Christ, commonly known as the Mormon church, which is based on the revelations received by the prophet, Joseph Smith, in the 1820s. Arising out of the East was the prophet, the Bab, the Gate, and his disciple who later became the prophet, Baha'u'llah, the founder of the Baha'i faith. The Baha'is claim to be the new universal religion and one of their tenets is the universality of mankind, the universality of all faiths.

As we have approached our century, however, everything has been greatly accelerated and the existence of the energy of mind and of intellect is functioning on our planet as never before. Something like eighty to ninety per cent of all the scientists who have ever lived in the history of mankind are alive right now.

All of this ferment seems to fulfil the ancient prophecies. Certainly we can look upon our world today and see that the prophecies of the Christ, when he said there will be wars and rumours of wars, there will be prophets and messiahs arising claiming to be the Christ, can be seen as definitely working out in our society. This lends great impact to the conviction of consciousness that we are now going to enter a new age. In the West, probably in the East as well, there has arisen within the past seventy to eighty years what can only be called a New Age movement.

I am not interested in the rather exotic cults and groups and messiah-types that emerge from the cauldron of human longing and human aspiration, but in what is needed to truly externalize a new age, and what under the name of the New Age movement may yet be hindering such a manifestation.

120

The first great hindrance, the first great facet of the jewel which *can* be a hindrance if misinterpreted, is prophecy. The second facet is the energy coming in under the Seventh Ray, which promotes the phenomenon of spiritual birth, the relationship between the soul and the personality, the relationship which occultly speaking is called the birth of the Christ.

Mankind throughout his history, at least throughout his recent history, the past two or three thousand years, has been very, very form-oriented. As he has become less sensitive psychically, with the closing down of man's mass psychic awareness in the days of very ancient cultures such as Atlantis, his attention has naturally gone much more to the concrete form of his world and the outer manifestation has become increasingly important. There are very good reasons for this in terms of the evolution of consciousness, because man must learn how to deal with form before he can truly be a creator.

What it has done is to give to most human cultures a value system that is firmly rooted in a perspective that says form is important, substance or the inner aspect is less important. This kind of value system is seen very much in our present society. Also, within the Western world at least, within fairly recent years, man's consciousness groping with the mystery and limitation of form has become somewhat enraptured by death. Man has always been rather death-conscious since the days when he lost his awareness that death was nothing more than just an easy stepping from one level to another.

Death in an occult sense does not exist. The closest thing to it is the entrapment in form, or any static state, any state which cannot grow, cannot move. The closest thing to it would be a frozen river, but a frozen river which was determined even in the presence of heat to remain frozen, consciousness doggedly determined to imprison itself in form. The spectre of death only exists in human consciousness because it is only the human mind with its power of free choice, coupled with his attunement to the forces of matter, which can create a condition in which we demand form above growth, a static state above a dynamic one. So man can create the true death and by creating it experience it.

When the Christ manifested himself, he manifested life abundant. Yet what we remember him best for is his death. We become quite fascinated with his ability to overcome that death, and through that very fascination we keep our attention riveted upon death itself. The Christian message became quite subtly distorted in that it became a message of survival rather than a message of life. We see this as well in certain modern movements such as spiritualism, which hold in their highest aspects a great potential for illumining human awareness, but in their usual manifestation are simply prostituted to a search for assurance—assurance that I as a personality will survive after death.

Now understand what this means. The whole concept of personal survival is based on a desire to die in an esoteric sense, because it means I am placing my personal identity—which is a form, a static state which I want to persist through eternity—above change, above growth. I want to be assured that when I leave this body I will persist, and I will persist in a way that is indestructible, and that nothing can then harm me; I am not then subject to the ravages of time and of circumstance, and I will not be forced to change. But as far as the soul is concerned that is death, that is non-life. So when we are talking about Christ as our personal saviour, what we may really be saying is, Christ is our personal slayer. We are attempting to use a concept of life to turn it into a state of death.

In the New Age movement, many people have decided that Christianity has ceased to 'fill the bill.' It no longer meets the needs of modern humanity. Something else must take its place, perhaps theosophy, perhaps esotericism under many schools such as the arcane school, perhaps one of the Eastern disciplines. Often what happens is that Jesus is simply replaced by another master and no real progress as far as basic fundamental conceptual change has occurred for the individual. There is this tendency to feel in the New Age movement that Christianity no longer is a viable proposition because it does not have the right language, it does not talk about things like reincarnation, the New Age, the Hierarchy, and so on.

These are important concepts, and one day they will be the foundation stones of a greater human science than we now have. But they are not intrinsically important. They are not so important as an understanding of what lies behind them. Many people in the New Age movement use reincarnation simply as a substitute for the Christian doctrine of survival to indicate that some aspect of their being continues on unchanged. They speak about previous lives as if indeed they were the same being who is reincarnating, whereas esoterically that is not so. The doctrine of reincarnation is far more subtle than that, and the being which you are at this moment has never existed on this planet in the form in which it is. The soul may have re-embodied itself, but each re-embodiment is unique and displays another facet of the eternal divine jewel of the being. The laws linking one life to another are far more subtle and complex than has yet been determined by the rather parlour room type of esotericism that is generally discussed.

Into all this consciousness of humanity which revolves around form, revolves around specific events and specific people and specific places, comes this fantastic enlivening energy, the idea of a new age, of a new birth for humanity, of a transition. Also there comes as a result of this various happenings in the phenomenal world which seem to reflect accurately prophecies of the past, and certainly encourage people to start making prophecies now. Probably fifty per cent of the people in the New Age movement, who are leaders in the movement, are prophets, and the majority of their prophecies seem to me to revolve around the concepts of destruction.

There is a truth in this. When you have living water that has been iced up, at some point the ice has to shatter and dissolve for the living stream to move again. And there is moving—in fact, it has been moving for over a hundred years—a force through our society which is a force of divine will which as it impacts within human culture is highly destructive. It is destructive because the old forms, the forms in which man has encased his life, must be shattered so that new life can emerge. It is no different than a snake shedding its skin.

But the New Age movement postulates, in many of its manifestations and understandings and teachings, the existence of a forthcoming event, an economic collapse, a war, the planet will tilt on its axis—something is going to happen which will release forces within the Earth which will transform the planet.

Now undoubtedly there is a truth embodied in this. Part of the truth however is ancient memory rather than present reality. For when man existed in the rather instinctual state of primitive man, or more primitive than he is now, such as in the Atlantean cultures, the only way in which man could undergo change once crystallization had set in was through planetary cataclysm. Cataclysm was the teaching method and the regenerative method which the guardians of the race employed, simply because humanity was not possessed at that time of sufficient self-initiative to do anything on its own to change the conditions. Like a child who is caught into a bad habit, the parent may have to step in and do something to change the child's environment, to alter the habit pattern, because the child is not mature enough or understanding enough to do it for himself.

There is an interesting prophecy or promise that was made, which is recorded in the Old Testament. It tells how after the flood God promised that never again would mankind be wiped out by a flood, but that the next time he would get it through fire. This statement is being widely interpreted in the New Age movement circles as meaning that we are wide open for a nuclear holocaust. But that is too obvious an interpretation. If there is anything I can say about the mind of God—and there are very, very few things I can say about it—it is that, for my money, he tends to be rather subtle.

Fire, esoterically, is energy. And fire has always referred occultly to the energy of the mind, the energy of the soul. The fire descending out of heaven is quite literally the energy of the soul moving into the personality through the link which we have been talking about, the birth of the Christ, a fire that is not destructive but highly stimulating.

It is destructive too, as all who are undergoing personality changes can testify. It puts you through your paces and demands the best of you; and at times on emotional and mental levels, even physical levels, you may feel as though you are burning up in one way or another. But this fire that is being applied to man is designed to stimulate his divine consciousness so that he himself initiates the changes which are required.

The three great divine centres of this planet are known as: one, Shamballa, which is not so much a place although it is often spoken of as being a place, but it is really a state of consciousness which is omnipresent, a state of consciousness representing the will of God; two, the Hierarchy, which is the heart centre of the planet representing the love of God; and three, the mass of humanity, the collective human soul and consciousness which represents the mind of God.

Never before has it been possible for these three centres to work in conjunction, simply because man has not been developed to the point where humanity could work as a united whole, or at least sufficient numbers of people could work in unity so that the latent creative energy within humanity could be harnessed for divine purposes. For that reason when changes needed to be done or initiated, they were initiated through other kingdoms, and men grew through responding to the effects—such as, initiating through the devic kingdom certain extreme planetary states, earthquakes, floods, and so on.

Now man can begin to assume the mantle of his own divine creativity and forge the new world. Do not underestimate the transforming power of this, because the civilization we have created in the past is by no means a soul-oriented civilization. It is death-oriented. It is form-oriented. It is security-oriented, security in the sense of clinging to form rather than clinging to spirit. As the fire of the soul descends from higher consciousness and begins to work through the minds and hearts of people, it is not going to stand by and brook any nonsense. It is highly, highly destructive in the occult sense of that term, because it is highly, highly constructive and building; and it will reflect into the environment the qualities of the soul. Any aspect, any institution, any tradition, any culture that reflects only the aspects of the personality will be consumed.

But that is an entirely different way of interpreting the prophecies than saying that something is going to occur, an event; and only those individuals who, through meditation, through study, through learning, through knowing the occult jargon, through joining groups, have proved themselves card-carrying members of the New Age movement, are going to survive and move into the new. So many things that are published and put out, both things that are being received from the higher planes, and things that are coming out from groups stress this factor of 'Let's get with it kids, because if you don't it is going to happen very soon and you won't make it!'

But that is nothing less than Christian survivalism dressed up in esoteric terms. It is saying to people: 'If you believe in the New Age and if you join this group or if you follow that master or if you practice this technique, then you, you as a form, you as an identity, will survive!' But that is nonsense. As soon as you open the door just a crack to the entry of your soul, you have signed your death warrant because you as a personality will cease to exist. You will be consumed. You will be transmuted. You will be changed. You will be transformed like a worm into a butterfly, into what you were designed to be, into what you are at all times. You will become a living soul. You will become a Christed being. You will become yourself.

With this energy that is stimulating people's contact with their soul levels it is not a pure contact at first, or even for some time after. If I am suddenly able to make a trans-Atlantic phone call to a dear friend of mine and I talk with them, I still am here. I am in Findhorn; I am surrounded with people I know, I am surrounded with the environment I am accustomed to. The fact of the phone call may make me very happy. It may give me news that I am pleased to have, but it does not really alter anything. It may, but it does not have to.

When I contact my soul and it begins to make itself known, I can rise and say, 'Oh jolly, happy day! What a splendid, beautiful experience,' and it can be exquisite. But I am still surrounded with thought patterns of my past, my conditioning, the thought patterns of other people in my environment, my culture, all of it. I can then, once I get to thinking about it and intellectualizing the experience or emotionalizing the experience, go right into the whole glamour of the thing. The soul is divine. When you touch it, you are touching God.

We must understand that the mind is the link. The gap between the mind—the lower mind as it relates to form—and the soul, is an incredible gap. It is like the gap between what the Christian thinks of as the individual and God. When the mind first encounters that and experiences this onrush of divinity, all kinds of things can begin to happen to that mind. If it is not careful it will begin thinking of itself as the messiah, or as a leader, or as the one who has grasped the truth and has a mission now to tell the world.

Now in a deep sense this is so. This is a valid thing because the messiah is a universal consciousness; and at some point each of us has to take up the responsibility, the burden if it is a burden, and the awareness of being a Christ unto our world, as long as we do it in perspective and with more than a good sense of humour about it, and realize that it is a group thing. We are in the company of many Christed beings, or potentially Christed beings. At the same time this can be misunderstood, and out of it arises groups and cults and individual idiosyncracies. I have met people who have come to see me, or have sat in my office, or talked with me, and they are trembling, waiting for me to recognize that they are the Christ. They have come that I might be one of the first to realize and take advantage of their divine mission.

It is a tremendous amount of energy, of validity, operating here, but being utilized to create more form rather than dissolving the form, symbolically speaking, freeing the consciousness so that it can become part of a group experience, a planetary experience, a cosmic experience. It can join the rhythm of life rather than setting itself apart from life and saying 'I am the one.'

This kind of thing, I feel, will balance out as more and more people begin to experience, and as more people who are in the know begin to realize that the most important thing for any person to establish in their consciousness now is what could be called the 3-D consciousness; by which I mean: discipline, discrimination, and disillusionment. If we have not become disillusioned yet, it is high time we started in the true sense which means seeing things as they are and not as we think they are, not dealing with an illusionary world. Discernment and discrimination move towards this. Discipline moves towards this, and these three qualities are essential for a person who would be a server of the race at this time. Such servers are needed. We are all needed.

The birth of the Christ is occurring. The great event for which the past two thousand years have largely been preparation, and about which prophecies have forewarned us, is happening all about us now. I recognize that undoubtedly there will continue to be upheavals and changes in the natural order of things, and in point of fact there is planned that at some date the continental structure of the Earth as we know it will undergo considerable change, but to the best of my understanding that is another two or three thousand years in the future, when suddenly America and Asia as we know them will cease to exist and new continents will take their place.

There will be these changes. The tragedy of the prophecies that are being proclaimed now is that again they are focusing consciousness where it has been focused, on what is happening in the world of form. They are making people wait, and by waiting they are not recognizing what is happening about them now—the reality of the New Age, the reality of the fire that is descending and transforming our world.

As time goes along, as magic and occultism and esotericism and astrology and all the various occult arts which are coming back into the fore, somewhat stimulated by the return of the Seventh Ray, the ray of ceremony and magic among other things, more and more people will undoubtedly be jumping on the New Age bandwagon. This idea of the New Age is incredibly potent, particularly as increasing numbers of young and older people become disgusted with the civilization that we have created. But the potency and indeed the sacredness of this idea is not that it is suddenly saying, 'Well, Big Daddy is now going to come and change things for us, and then we shall be happy in a New Age.' Its potency is that it is a call to the highest within us to suddenly throw off the shackles of glamour, of illusion, of waiting, of inertia, of despondency, of not seeing ourselves as we are, of not defining man as he can be and should be, and begin to externalize the building qualities that we have, begin to contribute through service, through awareness, through love, through wisdom, through right human relations, through more planetary consciousness, to the externalization of the new civilization.

Then the New Age movement will become what it is intended to be: the true vanguard of human evolution, the bridge building operation which will make it possible for man to move successfully from one level to another.

Another factor which is unfortunate about the prophetic word not properly understood or properly utilized is that it can be self-fulfilling and encourages people to think in terms of the death of the form rather than the life of the spirit. It can also be utilized as a licence to change. Ian Fleming created James Bond, 007. It meant he had a licence to kill, a chap who could go around shooting anybody he wanted to and he could get away with it. Ah, wish-fulfilment! In some ways some of the teachings concerning the New Age and the new energies and the necessity to destroy old forms can be interpreted in the same way: licence to destroy, licence to change without wisdom.

We are asked to be bridge builders, creators, drawing on the best of what man has created so that we can move on and create still better in the future. The concept of everything that evolution has created suddenly coming to a grinding stop and a new order taking over is in a fashion true, because evolution and form is only part of the story. There is such a thing as divine intervention and we are experiencing it now, but it is intervention within the law and the downflow of the human spirit. By the same token, that kind of consciousness which sees an abrupt end and a new beginning encourages either a waiting attitude or a fatalistic attitude or an attitude of: 'Well, none of it is worth it anyway, so I am free to rebel. I am free to knock down that institution or destroy that tradition or get rid of that culture!'

One of the great hindrances that the forces of light and of building have to work with now is the well-intentioned but misguided people who are trying to usher the New Age in by knocking down everything in sight. Because as Sir Thomas Moore said in the play, *A Man for all Seasons,* when he was being counselled to go against the law—when in pursuing Satan you destroy all the laws, and you attempt to capture Satan when you have destroyed all the laws, suddenly Satan turns on you. Then where is your protection?

There is an incredibly thin line between what is a force of light and a force of darkness. On some levels the line does not even exist at all. They are one and the same.

The New Age movement if seen in destructive terms can just as easily become an instrument for the enslavement of man as a herald of his liberation. People who see their task as being not one of building but of destroying may be and in fact are serving a certain divine purpose, but at the same time they can lay themselves directly open to being utilized by forces which they think they are working against. The people who are willing to kill for peace, for example.

So we are being blessed with the outpouring of an idea, an idea that has many facets. How we now grasp and utilize that idea will determine the ease or the difficulty of the transition that we are now making and will make. There is no question but that we will enter the New Age. The question is: can we do it in a relatively shorter period of time with a great deal of ease, or are we going to put ourselves through the mill?

We are faced with the challenge that centuries of the past have conditioned us to see the world in certain ways. We identify ourselves with the body, with the personality, therefore we are interested in survival. We identify the values of our world with form, and so we are interested in either destroying the form if we do not like it or trying to save it if we do.

The whole New Age idea is that we begin to see the reality behind form and work with that reality, let form adjust itself which it will do. The black magician is the man that works directly with the forces of matter and form. The white magician is the one who works with the forces of the soul. The black magician invokes the elementals to do his will. The white magician works directly with the devas and the angelic kingdoms. He works in cooperation with them, does not attempt to bend them to his will. Since he establishes a cooperative relationship, when a deva moves towards an end that a human consciousness has established, all the elementals who are under that deva's control will move accordingly.

In this time, then, we come to the crisis of how will we use the magic of the Seventh Ray. Will it be prostituted into what if not black is at least grey, because we are using it to maintain the kind of consciousness that we have had for a number of centuries now, building a new age on rotten foundations? Or will we turn and begin to learn the true meaning of magic, the white magic of the soul, the magic of that transforming fire which acts within the individual; first to change his and her life to make it more balanced, more wise, more disciplined, more discriminating, more loving, more open, more aware, and then to work in harmony and cooperation with the souls of others?

That is the idea that is moving. That is the New Age movement. Nothing that man creates is a New Age movement unless it is the soul of man from which it springs. That soul is now becoming very, very active. For the fire that was promised is descending upon us. And as this activity increases our potential, our magical potential also increases. Our potential for energizing this movement increases. Then we increasingly become faced with the choice of how we will use what we are being given.

Chapter Ten

Architects of Aquarius

There are three major centres which affect evolution upon this planet, three centres of power or influence or energy. One of these is called Shamballa. Although it does have a spacial location in the Gobi desert, this is not a place as much as it is a state of consciousness; that state, that awareness, that presence in which the will of God is known. The purposeful intent of the creator for this planet is known and that intent is itself a living energy.

The second centre is what is called the Hierarchy or the Communion of Saints, or the White Brotherhood, or the Masters of Compassion and Wisdom. They have many names but they represent those beings both human and non-human or devic, who have evolved out of humanity or out of the deva evolution, and have achieved a state of God consciousness or illumination.

The third great centre is the centre of humanity. Always before in human history the will to change and the energy that effects change has emerged from the first two centres: will coming from Shamballa, love-wisdom energy coming from the Hierarchy. The mind or the intelligence aspect which humanity is destined to unfold and make manifest has not been so prevalently expressed. Quite literally man was not evolved enough to make the necessary changes all by himself to transform his world. But that condition is now changing. Man now is at a point where a signficiant number of the race can take on themselves the burden, if burden it is, or the responsibility or the challenge or the joy of being the instrument of divine intelligence which blended with love, with wisdom and with creative will can transform the planet. No longer then does the burden lie upon the overlords of planetary evolution. It is at least partly shared, and perhaps to a great extent shared by humanity.

This is the most significant aspect of this New Age. Past ages when transformation has occurred or revelation has been given have been inaugurated by an individual or by a very small group of individuals. This age is different. There may be individuals manifesting. There may be and probably will be another physical manifestation of an avatar, an illumined being, representing the head of the Hierarchy; but the significant manifestation of transforming energy is going to emerge from the corporate consciousness of humanity itself. That is both our destined glory and our opportunity.

We are being asked in this age not only to be experiencers and observers of change but actual architects of change, those who can grasp the plan of the master builder and bring that plan down into externalization with intelligence, with right use of free will, with wisdom, with love and with purposeful intent, or illumined will. We are asked to be architects of Aquarius.

The ancient prophecies which tend to relate to our time, particularly prophecies dealing with destruction, emerge from an age and from a consciousness when humanity was not yet at a point where it could all by itself take on the burden of creative transformation. It was primarily through divine intervention that transformation was brought about. Cataclysm was the method of change in those days, and it is only logical to realize that when the ancient consciousnesses sought to interpret the events as best they could perceive them within the mind of God, they interpreted them within the context of their understanding. We are now having to deal with their interpretation. In some cases the way in which we deal with it will determine exactly how easily we can make the transition from one age to another. For prophecies have a definite way of being self-fulfilling, and if a great number of people are convinced that the world will undergo certain kinds of changes in a certain specific fashion, then indeed the world will undergo those changes in that fashion.

The purpose of this book is not so much to tell you how we are going into the New Age as much as it is to give you the vision, some suggestions as to what it is all about. No one person could say *how* we are going to go into the New Age, because that is emerging now through the centre that we call humanity, in conjunction and cooperation with the love and will aspect of the divine.

However there are some things that we can say. In the last chapter I spoke about the 3-Ds which every good disciple can learn, in fact must learn: discipline, discrimination and disillusionment. These three have been taught to man through the ages. Through Moses came the law of discipline, admittedly expressed in a negative fashion. It is a law expressed in terms of don'ts, but none the less Moses was the great avatar of the law, or one of the great avatars of the law. Through the Buddha we have discernment and discrimination, and he taught the way of balance and the noble Eightfold Path. Through Christ, through the power of the love, wisdom and will aspects which he manifested, comes the potentiality of disillusionment, by which I simply mean the ability to see clearly into the reality behind form. For example, Christ supposedly demolished the great illusion of death by demonstrating his resurrection. I say supposedly only because the majority of Christians still tend to believe that there is such a thing as death, and believe that Christ and belief in Christ is a way of surviving death. Whereas a person who really understands what Christ manifested realizes that there is only the transforming principle of the divine, that life itself is indeed eternal.

Our builders need to know the 3-Ss: silence, service, synthesis. These are three keys to the New Age consciousness. First, silence. Silence means a good deal more than keeping one's mouth shut. Silence is a state of consciousness, a state of inner rhythm. It is not necessarily a state of non-activity. A person may be very active but at the same time be very quiet and very silent.

Silence is the well-spring of creativity. It is the point of perspective. It is the centre where the will of God is known and from where man can draw the love and wisdom and intelligence required to externalize that will.

Silence is timelessness. It means in the press of daily events, the pressures of daily challenge, taking time to look and to listen and to see clearly and to hear clearly. Silence is essential to communication. In fact if you attempt to communicate to someone who is not silent, the chances are very little communication will take place. The person who is listening does not just have to be quiet in terms of speech, but he needs to be quiet in terms of thought. For we have all had the experience of talking to someone who is not saying anything in return, but we can tell that their mind is a million miles away where he is carrying on some internal conversation with beings or being invisible.

Silence is where it all begins. If we are to grasp as architects the plans, the blueprint that God is providing, then at some point we have to learn the discipline of silence, and the peace of silence. This may involve learning meditation. Different people meditate in different ways. That is why I have never taught a meditative technique. But it is important to seek out some kind of technique, or some kind of approach to timelessness, to silence; something that you can feel comfortable with. It may be sitting quietly at a certain time of the day, each day, and establishing a rhythm. It may be through doing certain things that occupy your attention and allow you to focus on that activity and become silent in activity. Whatever rhythm seems right to you, it is still important that silence be understood and applied. All creative things emerge from silence.

Silence again is a presence. It is a state of being. It is itself dynamic. It is not passivity necessarily. Silence also implies learning how to speak correctly. We are told that one of the sciences of the New Age will be the science of sound and speech. This has always been an occult science, the use of sound, mantrums, various kinds of chants, sacred words, to effect changes in the environment. That is one of the foundation stones of magic. The power of right speech which is one of the eight of the Eightfold Path that Buddha taught, is directly akin to the power of creativity. 'In the beginning was the Word, the Word was with God, the Word was God.' God spoke and the things that he said took form. That is essentially true with us as well. We speak, and what we say takes form in one way or another, even if that form is only in our attitude. Like it or not, we do listen to ourselves when we talk and since we are generally our own best listeners we also tend to believe whatever we say. So silence implies right use and understanding of speech, when to talk and when not to talk, what to say and when not to say it.

Service. Service is a keynote for the New Age. Service in the New Age is not an ideal. In the Piscean age men glamorized the concept of service and in fact sought to serve the ideal of service. This has been a very good thing for out of this has come many great and philanthropic institutions. The Christian religion which holds forth the ideal of brotherly love and service has given to the world hospitals, schools, homes for the elderly and for the infirm and for orphans and so on. Men have joined societies, have joined brotherhoods, have joined institutions dedicated to service because this was the thing to do.

But a great deal of service is given because we feel it is right to serve, not necessarily because service is needed, nor even necessarily because we know exactly what is needed. It takes a great deal of true wisdom and discrimination to know exactly what kind of service is required in a situation or by a person.

Sometimes the best service that can be given is no service at all. Let that person get on with it. One of the tasks of a spiritual teacher, for example, may often be to promote into the life of a disciple a condition of great challenge which may bring suffering to the disciple, and the teacher then has to stand aside and watch that person suffer and not take steps to interfere. A teacher who understands and who truly loves can do this because after all suffering only happens to forms. It does not happen to the soul. It does not happen to the spirit. It does not happen to the inner man. As soon as the person wakes up to that fact he stops suffering. It is the great thing that Buddha taught and that Jesus demonstrated.

Service, though it is a keynote of the New Age, needs to be understood in terms of the New Age, in terms of using one's mind, one's intellect, warmed by the fires of the heart, filled with compassion but not with sympathy, to determine how best to give right service. It requires discrimination. It requires true love. It requires often courage. Service none the less will become, and is becoming, the most important outflow of life to life. We will see in the years ahead, as the New Age energies come increasingly into play, a greater and greater emphasis upon true service—not upon serving to meet one's own need to serve, or one's own glamorous ideal of what service should be, but because one recognizes the true need and then opens oneself for the divine to flow through to meet the need. Service thus proceeds from silence, from a state of quiescence, of balance, of perspective.

The third S is synthesis. This too is a hallmark of the New Age. Synthesis is the next higher manifestation of analysis. Man is an analytical being, speaking generally. His evolutionary path has been one to develop the qualities of emotion and mind in dealing with duality and in separation and diversity. But as we enter the age of Aquarius, what we are asked to build demands unity, wholeness.

Synthesis does not mean sameness. It does not mean conformity. It

137

does mean the ability for disparate and separate elements to learn to work harmoniously.

A concept which is very much used now in a lot of social and political literature is the concept of synergy. Synergy simply means a state in which energy is produced through the union of many different elements. A synergetic society is one in which all the elements of the society work together for the good of each element. A non-synergetic society is one in which each element of the society works for its own good at the expense of other elements, in essence a competitive society.

An example of synergy at work would be to have four or five people with different ideas about how something should be done, coming together and instead of competing, they blend their ideas and out of their synthesis together comes not a compromise, not a sacrifice on someone's part, but a deeper, greater understanding which creates a new pattern in which no one loses. For that matter no *one* person wins. Everyone in a synergetic situation wins because everyone is benefited.

Synthesis is definitely Seventh Ray manifestation. It is built up out of communication. It creates ordered activity. It creates working together. It is the life-blood of New Age group endeavour. In the past groups have developed basically in two fashions: either around a strong centre point or individual so that what we really have is the master-group situation, or the leader-group situation; or the group has developed around an ideal in which you have the group as being all important and the individual units of the group are important only in so far as they are part of the group. This is the tyranny of the group and we see it expressed in certain manifestations of totalitarianism within our planet where the state is placed above the individual.

But the group consciousness in the New Age is one of synthesis and synergy. The group may collect around a crystal point, a seed point, an individual or a core group who embody the basic idea of the group, but that core group or individual is in essence no more important than any other individual in the group. The group consciousness is the united product of all of them, of each person blending his or her contribution to the whole.

In order for this to be done each person has to unfold sufficiently to have something meaningful to contribute. The synergetic group, the New Age group, is dependent upon the existence of self-fulfilling or self-actualizing or enhanced individuals. If one wishes to be an architect of Aquarius, he must learn to stand in silence within himself, be able to look upon what is happening in the world and not react emotionally or mentally, with glamour, with illusion; he must be able to look upon the atrocities of Northern Ireland or Vietnam or the Middle East; he must be able to look upon pollution, upon traffic jams, upon nine-to-five work shifts six days a week; he has to be able to look on all of it from a position of silence, because there is his strength. If the world makes him react, he is an extension of the world. He may be able to do good work up to a point but his work is only in reaction to an apparent need, not in divine movement towards a true need; because the ills of the world that we see are only symptoms, they are not the cause.

He must learn silence, non-reactivity, discrimination. He must see from that point where he can give service and how it seems best to him to give it, and open himself to a willingness that it is not *he* who shall give the service. It is not 'Oh boy, me now, who has a chance to fulfil this great role in the divine plan and give service!', it is a divinity that is going to give the service. When a person really knows that he is divine, that exercise is not important any more because he knows that he is giving a service but he is selfless about it at the same time.

You know when you have hit that point. There is no question about it. You know it because largely you have forgotten it and you are able to respond with love and with wisdom to what needs doing. The individual must learn how to synthesize himself with others.

Here we come to the great meaning of the Seventh Ray as the ray of ceremonial magic. The white magic is the magic of the soul and the soul is a manifestation of group awareness. For the soul is love without limit. It does not differentiate itself into the self and the not-self. On the level of the soul, the divine, there is only the one. There is no loss of individuality but still just the one. The magic of the soul is the magic of making that oneness apparent in its affairs. Therefore the magic of the New Age is the ceremony of right human relations, communication, communion, community. How can I best learn to relate to the people in my immediate environment? How can I build harmony, peace, understanding with them?

Then perhaps I can learn how to build it on much greater levels. This means awareness. How can I establish right relations with the tools with which I work, the environment in which I must work, with the things that I must use? For these things also have life, mineral life, plant life, animal life.

How can I relate myself as a son of God to my world? That is the ceremonial challenge of consciousness in the New Age.

To be an architect of Aquarius means accepting one factor about the New Age: that it is not just happening, *I* am helping to make it happen. Yes, there are energies coming from the other great centres, the Hierarchy and Shamballa, which will cause things to happen on the Earth. We are seeing a lot of these things happen, upheavals here and changes there. But that is not all by itself the New Age. The New Age now is a three-pronged effort, not a two-pronged effort, and if we simply wait for the other two builders to do their thing, we will have missed the significance of what the New Age means. For it means the initiation of man out of a state of spiritual dependency into the state of spiritual maturity and Christhood, where he can at long last in significant numbers begin to wear the mantle of responsibility to his world and say 'I too am a creator on this planet, and as a son of God I can fulfil my creative responsibility.'

It is not enough to be aware of prophecy or to be aware of great energies moving from other dimensions as guided by the Hierarchy, or whatever. I must know what is happening to me as an individual. What am I experiencing emotionally, mentally? How can I transform it into that which is a blessing to my world? Let me not say, 'Well, I don't know how to do this,' because we have had plenty of training down the ages. Buddha taught us. Jesus taught us. It is available in teachings of people now. It is there if we choose to look for it. But even more importantly it is there if we choose to act on it.

That is where the missing link has been, the lack of true, intelligent, wise action. We have idealized the spiritual life and worshipped it. In the New Age we must utilize it as a tool and build with it. Spiritual life is our magical instrument by which we as divine magicians can transform our planet. This is the New Age vision: what man is capable of and what man will become because of his own self-initiated efforts in harmony with the aid that he is being given from other sources.

A new age dawns upon the Earth. The call goes forth above the clamour and battle sounds of Armageddon, that now there will be peace on Earth and good will flowing between men, for now is the age of the birth of the Christ within the heart of humanity.

As this call sounds, will we respond? The blueprint is unfolded upon the table of our hearts and of our minds. All of our universe ask us this question, 'Man, individually, collectively, will you respond and become an architect of Aquarius?'

Chapter eleven

The Loins of Aquarius

In the Old Testament quite often God speaks to the prophets and says, 'Gird up thy loins and go . . . here or there or some place else,' to carry out his will. Generally he sends them off into the desert or to some city that is having a great time in sin and despair to preach repentance. It is a very common phrase throughout the Old Testament, to gird up one's loins and to set forth.

We are each of us latter-day prophets who are being asked to do that: to gird up our loins, go forth into the world and become architects of Aquarius. I find that this is a very fascinating phrase, very symbolic. It means more than just putting on one's trousers and getting ready to sally forth into the desert or to the cities. It really means to harness one's creative powers, to bring one's creative energies to a peak of accessibility and of focusing so that they can be released in service, released in building. We are each of us the creative potential inherent in the world, a creative potential that is now being asked to be released that a new age can be born.

When we begin to build something, it is often with a very special kind of consciousness. Suppose you were given a piece of land and you were told that upon this land you could build your home. You would go to an architect and you would enlist his service. With his help you would draft out a plan for your home: how you wished your rooms to be arranged, how you wished your garden to be landscaped. All of this is very exciting and you are filled with a sense of anticipation and pleasure and joy as the home begins to take shape, especially if you are privileged to take part in the actual building of it. This enhances your sense of joy and creativity. The consciousness of a builder is a consciousness of anticipation and of excitement and a sense of accomplishment.

During the Renaissance when people in Europe were seized by this great creative fervour, they would go forth and begin to build these mammoth works of art that were the great cathedrals. These were tasks which no one man could hope to see completed in his lifetime. Whole generations would be involved in a given area of work. A given skill, a certain skill of masonry or of stone sculpture or of woodworking, would be passed from father to son. Where the father had worked on the scaffolding the son would take his place and work on the scaffolding, and this tradition of building was passed on through generations. Imagine the consciousness involved in knowing that I will not see my work completed but my son, and my son's sons will. They will carry on after me. Even though I will not see the finished product, I still have enough pride and joy and pleasure from my work that I will give my all to it. I will gird up my creative powers and bring them to this point of consecration to accomplishing the task at hand.

Within us each lies that which is timeless. It was present before the foundations of the Earth. It was present when, within the creative imagination of the Divine, the image was formed and held of this planet and all of its destiny. It was present when the first bits and pieces of cosmic dust began to coalesce. It was present when molten rock heaved in great seas of geological upheaval and then cooled to become the mountains and the plains. It was present as the rains fell and the oceans were created and life emerged from those oceans. This consciousness will be present when the Earth has accomplished its task and falls spinning back into its molten source and becomes again one with the Sun.

In our everyday consciousness we see with the eyes of a vastly reduced time scale. Our vision is narrowed and is measured not by light-years, not by mega-years, not by eons of time; it is measured by minutes and by seconds and by days and hours and years. We say that we shall live for three score years and ten, and then we depart to penetrate what to man at his present stage of awareness remains the great mystery of life beyond form. Yet throughout this life with its narrow focus of vision there remains within us that timeless consciousness which has grasped all the seasons of the Earth and which knows the seasons yet to come, and because of that grasp and that knowledge cannot be affected by change that is born of minutes but can only respond to change which spans the eons.

Our source centre, our divinity, which we call the soul—I am sometimes asked if the soul and the spirit are the same. Fundamentally speaking, no they are not, they are two different levels of consciousness, but for our purposes I am lumping them together and simply calling it the soul—within that level, within that consciousness, the plan is known. It is not known in the same way that one would read a book and see from that handbook what must be done; for example, how to build a fire or how to read a compass. It is known because the soul *is* the plan.

When you are facing your first bit of land and have the opportunity to build your home on it, you may go to an architect to have the plans drawn up. Where do those plans come from? They are coming from you. They are coming from your concept of what a home is. And that is born from many things. It is born from your past experience of a home, the home you had with your parents perhaps, a home that you have dreamed of through the years, the home that you have conceived of as being that place in which your creative ideas could find fulfilment. When you plan your rooms you plan them in terms of your hopes and dreams, your expectations: this will be my study where I can relax, and read and write; or this will be my sewing room, or this will be my art studio, this will be the family room where I can create an environment of peace for my loved ones, this will be the kitchen where my love can pour into the creation of nourishment.

Plans take shape, but these plans emerge from a complex centre within you that is itself combining many levels of experience, past, future, present, in order to come up with that abstraction that you call home. From that abstraction you plan your physical form and hope that to the best of its ability that physical form will be a suitable vehicle through which that abstraction can take form.

So it is with God. So it is with our own divinity. That which is the source of man's future, the source of the plan, is not a blueprint. It is not a set of ancient tablets on which the whole thing was pre-written. It is something which is beyond words, beyond form, but none the less real because of it.

When you sit down to plan out your future, you plan your future on the basis of what you have been taught, of what you have been led to expect, what you hope to see. Yet if you really think about it, you can trace your planning back to a centre within yourself which seems strangely divorced from physical plane experience. Where do your hopes come from? What is the fountainhead of your dreams?

We stand at the beginning of a new age, and the call comes out to us to gird ourselves and to become the creators of this new age. For many people this is a thought filled with bewilderment and trepidation because we are accustomed to relying upon experts to show us how to do things or to show us the way to go. We are accustomed in building our homes, for example, to go to an architect. On a physical level this is quite right, because I do not have the information concerning stress and engineering tensions and the relationship of various forms and building materials that would be necessary to insure that once I put up my roof it does not come crashing down on my head again.

But when we come to the matters of the spirit, there is only one expert and that is the divine, and the divine is essentially within us each. Certainly the divine is more apparent within some than within others. There are individuals who come into life with the mission to be points of focus around which great creative energies can coalesce and take form. But how do they take form if it is not through the lives of individuals who themselves respond to a call more penetrating than time and more powerful than individual hesitancy and limitation?

Can you believe that the New Age, its patterns, its forms, its destiny, lies within you? If you can believe this then you have taken the first major step towards ensuring that the New Age will be made manifest. You have taken the first step in girding up your loins and going forth to fulfil the will of the divine. For the first step, really, in any journey is knowing where to look.

There is a little booklet called *One Solitary Life* which is generally circulated about Christmas time. It is the story of Jesus. The theme of this booklet is how this one individual who according to historical records at any rate, never travelled any further than thirty miles from the place of his birth, and who only contacted comparatively minor numbers of people in his lifetime—whether that is actually historically correct or not that can be debated by people, but that is what the exoteric records tell us—how this one individual who had such restricted contacts with life in terms of vast communication and travel completely transformed the world.

How did he transform the world? Imagine a Jesus coming to the Earth and no one listening to him, not even one person! Suppose that he had said to Matthew, 'Follow me,' and Matthew had said, 'Well, I'd really rather not. I don't think I will today.' Or suppose he had said to Peter, 'Go forth and be fishers of men,' and Peter had said, 'Well, but men don't fetch a very high price on the market; I think I'll stick to carp' or cod or mackerel, or whatever one gets from the Sea of Galilee.

Jesus himself expressed this in his parable of the sowing of the seeds. Some seeds fall on rocky ground, and some fall on areas where weeds are growing, but a few seeds fall on fertile ground. Well, suppose he did not have any fertile ground. Someone has to respond. An avatar, after all, can only do so much. He can only be a point of focus through which certain energies can be released, certain truths enunciated; and then it takes, astonishingly enough, ordinary everyday run-of-the-mill people, what is so often called the mass, as if the mass had any existence, to respond, to provide the fertility of consciousness, to actually seize upon a message, to hear a word, to gird up their loins and to go forth and do something about it.

The brain can send messages to the body, but unless there is a backbone, a spinal cord, to carry the messages to the various appropriate centres, the brain can holler and scream all day and nothing is going to happen. Humanity is the backbone of the Earth. Humanity is the salt of the Earth. There is no such thing as an ordinary person. There is only God, life, the one consciousness manifesting through many, many forms: physical, emotional and mental forms. It is this one life in its many forms that must respond to itself and reveal itself.

The New Age is here. The new dispensation is upon us. For that matter, the second coming is upon us. For the light and life and spirit of the Christ, of the Divine, is moving through human consciousness in revelation.

Its movement must be within human consciousness through people who realize their affinity with the Divine, their attunement to God, and people who can begin to grasp this wondrous fact that the birth of the New Age is springing forth from within me. I have the choice to be fertile ground or non-fertile ground. I have the choice to be open to the teachings of the new as and when they come, and the teachings of the past as they have been given. I have the choice to make those teachings real, to externalize them. In other words,

I can be an architect of Aquarius. My life can help to set the pattern, can reveal the plan. The plan is not something that I have to read, it is something that I must be, that I can be to some extent, if only a minor one.

In our age, since it is a transitional age and all transitional ages tend to manifest the spirit of the destroyer, a great divine energy which sweeps through affairs in order to cleanse and to remove forms which have served their purpose and clear the way for new patterns to take shape. It is easy to look upon this process as it manifested within our world and to become convinced that, in some fashion, nothing seems to be going right. The world instead of responding to the great messages of truth and light and love and wisdom, which are man's spiritual heritage, seems instead to be responding ever more powerfully to messages of separation and hatred and destruction, fear, torment and anxiety.

If we are to be architects of the New Age, let us have the consciousness of the builder. Let us have the individual who says, 'Yes, my life is a creative adventure,' because it is! Your soul is creating itself. Your soul is creating its part and rhythm in the divine plan, and like any builder I can view this with joy, with anticipation, with excitement, with love. Just that kind of consciousness alone adds so much to one's world and one's environment.

When we think of world service, we tend to think: what are we doing to help world problems like Ireland, or Vietnam, or the Middle East crisis? But I am a world problem, and you are a world problem, and your neighbours are world problems. The world is that which surrounds us. So the place to begin solving world problems is in our own consciousness, and then in our immediate world and affairs. Then if necessary the paths will open for us to have influence, conscious influence, knowing influence, over what we usually call world affairs.

Those individuals who worked upon the great cathedrals in France, Germany and England, some of whom knew that they would not live to see their completion, nevertheless did not allow that sense of personal termination to deter them from the full application and release of their creative power. They did not say, 'Well, it's too late for me, this cathedral is for younger people, people who can start at an early age and see its completion.'

The cathedral of the New Age, the temple of man, the temple of God-man is being built now. The cornerstones have been laid. We are now in the process of building the superstructure.

Those who are what is commonly known as the older citizens often state, 'Well, I'm not really sure how much I can do in the time that is remaining, but you are fortunate because you are young and obviously the New Age is for you.' I wish to make it very, very clear that the New Age has nothing to do with time-age. The New Age is not a time-thing. It is a condition of attunement. The New Age has nothing to do with how much time you can put in, because the temple that we are building we are building always. We have been building it for millennia. We will continue building it. The few years that you are encased in physical form simply means that you are working on a different level of the scaffolding. When you leave physical form you are still working on the same building, you are just on a different level. Your work does not cease. Your creative opportunities do not cease. Your growth does not cease. That which you learn, even if you learn it five minutes before unfolding into a higher dimensional existence, is not lost nor is it a wasted time.

The New Age is the product of the release of collective attunement, of people affirming the principles of good will between men, of light released upon the Earth, of the promise of man, the heritage of man, the glory of man united with his Beloved. The New Age is not for a particular generation though the forms of it may be. It is for humanity. Whether you are in this dimension or any other, you are part of humanity.

In the past, whenever great changes have taken place upon the Earth, mankind was not in a position always to help initiate those changes. Generally he simply suffered through them. The changes had to be initiated for him by external forces, divine forces, and the transition points between past ages have quite often been marked by catastrophe, for example the flood. Now man is at a point where he himself must be the agent of the creative change, not simply endure the change or pass through it. He must create it. He must cause it. He must cooperate with the Divine in bringing the new heaven and the new Earth to birth.